Deaf Studies in Irє
An introductior

Deaf Studies in Ireland
An introduction

Edited by

PATRICK MCDONNELL

Douglas McLean

COLEFORD • ENGLAND

First published in 2004

Douglas McLean

8 St John Street
Coleford
Gloucestershire GL16 8AR
England
www.ForestBooks.com

British Library Cataloguing in Publication Data
A catalogue record for this book is available from the British Library
ISBN 0-946252-57-2

Typeset in 10.5/14pt Monotype Albertina
Printed in Great Britain by The Cromwell Press, Trowbridge, Wiltshire.
Typography and cover by Ernst Thoutenhoofd

Contents

Foreword

The past quarter of a century has witnessed a revolution in the Irish Deaf community's perception of itself. Since 1981 the Irish Deaf Society has been tireless in the pursuit of basic human rights for Deaf[1] people, especially official recognition for their distinctive language and culture and full access to education and all other institutions and processes of Irish society. Largely as a result of these efforts the same period has seen the beginnings—but so far only the beginnings—of a revolution in Irish society's perception of the Deaf community. For example, the Department of Education and Science has granted de facto recognition to Irish Sign Language, the Higher Education Authority has established a Centre for Deaf Studies in Trinity College Dublin, and hearing people have shown an increased interest in learning ISL. These and other developments are supported by the beginnings of research into ISL, Deaf history and culture, and the treatment of the Irish Deaf community by Irish society at large. Drawing on each of these strands, this book gives grounds for celebrating recent achievements, while providing timely reminders of a shameful past and plentiful indications of just how much remains to be done.

The first four papers in the collection offer insights into various aspects of Deaf experience. David Breslin's biographical sketches of five Deaf artists remind us that Deaf men and women have made a memorable contribution to Ireland's artistic and cultural heritage. One of them, Thomas Mahon, applied his gifts to the education of Deaf boys, creating a large number of instructional charts, some of which can be seen today in St Joseph's Heritage Centre. We cannot know how these Deaf artists communicated with their hearing clients, but it seems possible that at least some of them were less marginalized than those educated in the schools for the Deaf have so often been.

Helena Saunders gives a poignant account of what it was like to grow up Deaf in 1950s Ireland and to receive an education shaped by oralism. This curious doctrine, adopted here in the late 1940s, paid much greater attention to the mechanics of speech production than to the communication of meaning, which inevitably limited Deaf learners' access to the curriculum. As Helena Saunders testifies, in the heyday of oralism pupils were physically punished for using sign language. But predictably such cruelty had little effect; for the urge to communicate is one of the defining characteristics of humanity, and for members of the Deaf community communication means signing.

The use of corporal punishment to discourage Deaf pupils from signing is, of course, a thing of the past. But removing physical cruelty from educational institutions does not in itself improve the educational prospects of pupils and students. Carmel Grehan shows that in our own day Deaf access to public examinations still leaves a great deal to be desired. In a survey of eight Deaf people who have sat public examinations, four in 1980 or before and four between 1997 and 2000, she found little evidence of progress over the past forty years as regards Deaf students' access to the examinations. This situation seems unlikely to change until the Department of Education and Science takes account of the fact that written English—the medium through which students are mostly examined—is a second language for Deaf students.

The first section of the book ends on a more positive note than this, however, with a paper by Patrick Matthews and Susan Cave-Foley that offers a wealth of insights into Deaf community and culture. The paper reminds us that the Irish Deaf community is not a monolith but comprises individuals and families scattered across the country. It explains how membership of the community works and provides important guidance for hearing people unused to associating with their Deaf fellows. It also provides evidence of a rich linguistic and cultural inventiveness—two non-PC jokes are particularly to be savoured.

One of the things that makes Deaf people different, of course, is the fact that their language is manual-visual rather than vocal-auditory. This difference of channel is responsible for different modes of language processing and different kinds of linguistic structure. These are the concerns of the two papers that comprise the second section of the book. Dawn Duffin takes as her starting point the definition of 'psycholinguistics' given in a widely used dictionary of linguistics: 'the study of the mental processes underlying the planning, production, perception and comprehension of speech'—a definition that excludes sign languages. She then explores some of the key issues in language processing, taking account of sign language as well as speech. Her conclusion is unsurprising: in some respects the processing of sign language is similar to the processing of speech because both are shaped by the human faculty for language; in other respects, however, differences in channel give rise to differences in processing.

Patrick McDonnell's account of three verb categories—'agreement', 'plain' and 'classifier'—provides an accessible introduction to the linguistic description and analysis of the verb in ISL. Even readers unfamiliar with the formal study of language will gain a clear sense of some of the ways in which ISL structures and communicates meaning. They will also recognize that an enormous amount of work remains to be done before we can claim to have an adequate grammatical description of ISL.

If we are to work against the marginalization of the Deaf and find ways of connecting their language and culture to the language and culture of the hearing community, what paths do we need to follow in the future? The third section of the book provides some answers to this question. Joe McDonnell explores bilingualism with particular reference to deafness, discussing bilingual abilities, bilingualism and cognition, bilinguals in society, bilingualism and language planning, and bilingualism in education. His paper carries the strong implication that especially in terms of education and access, further progress will depend on recognizing and responding to the fact that Deaf people are bilingual.

In a comparative study of the Deaf communities of Ireland and Finland John Bosco Conama shows that although the two countries and their Deaf communities have much in common, since the 1980s a coherent strategy based on three policy strands—language, education and communication—has enabled the Finnish Deaf community to achieve significant gains. In the last few years Ireland has begun to catch up, thanks to the increased empowerment of the Irish Deaf community, though the Deaf remain largely excluded from the formulation of policy. Clearly, we have much to learn from the Finns in this regard.

Finally, Lorraine Leeson traces the history of attitudes to sign languages in the European Union and the Council of Europe, highlighting two significant recent developments: the inclusion of linguistic rights in the European Union's Charter of Fundamental Rights and the call made in the Council of Europe's Parliamentary Assembly for the same protections to be offered to sign languages as to regional and minority spoken languages. Both developments reflect a commitment to unity in diversity that is the only appropriate political basis for attempting to meet the many needs implied by this illuminating and engrossing collection.

David Little
Centre for Language and Communication Studies
Trinity College
Dublin

Note

1. In this book the term 'Deaf' is used to refer to deafness in a cultural sense; where the context is audiological or where cultural associations are not evident, the term 'deaf' is used—Editor's note.

Acknowledgment

The editor and publisher would like to thank the following for permission to reproduce copyright material: The Deaf Heritage Centre, St. Joseph's, Cabra, Dublin 7, for examples of the work of Thomas Mahon; the Russell family for examples of the work of Beatrice Gubbins.

I ASPECTS OF DEAF EXPERIENCE

Deaf lives in Ireland

David Breslin

Introduction

As a Deaf historian I have been conducting research since 1968 on the history of Deaf lives, particularly the lives of those connected with the arts in Ireland. In this chapter, for example, we might consider the life and work of John Duff, engraver, born in Dublin sometime between 1730 and 1740, who died in 1787 and was probably buried in St Werburgh's Church graveyard, not far from his business shop in Exchange Street; or the life and work of John Burns, born about 1740 and a native of Monaghan. Burns has a place in Deaf history as the earliest known Irish Deaf author. In 1775 he published a classic in Irish literary history, *An Historical and Chronological Remembrancer*, which had over 1,000 subscribers. A copy is kept in the Gilbert library in Dublin.

We might also look at the life and work of Francis McDonnell, another Dubliner, who was born in Francis Street in 1822, the son of a poor shoemaker. McDonnell first worked as a sculptor and later went to London from where he sent his painting, *The First Born*, to be shown at the Royal Hibernian Academy of Arts Exhibition in 1852. Although we know little else about his career, perhaps some day other works of his will be discovered.

Another interesting, though less well known Deaf artist was Francis Ross Maguire. Maguire, whose father was the talented history and portrait painter Thomas H. Maguire, was born in London in 1860 and may even have received an early start to his career from his father's teaching at home. His parents sent Francis to St. Joseph's School for Deaf Boys and his deaf sister to St. Mary's in Cabra, to receive a Catholic education. After their education they both returned to London. Francis worked there for the religious publications firm, Burns, Gill & Oates, but visited St. Joseph's for the annual mission and to meet his old classmates. He stayed in Cabra from 1912 to 1915 and during that time completed several murals which can still be seen in St. Joseph's. Unforunately, his large chart of the single- and double-handed manual alphabets, painted in white on black canvas and framed in a heavy black moulding was scandalously burned by the school authorities in 1978.

If our interest was writing rather than art we could turn to the life of Charlotte Grace O'Brien. Charlotte and her brother Willy were two deaf children in a family of eight whose father was William Smith O'Brien, the Irish Protestant nationalist and leader of the Young Ireland rebellion at Ballingarry, Co. Tipperary, in 1848. Charlotte became a novelist and social reformer. She took a large house in Queenstown (now Cobh) in Cork and registered as a lodging house keeper in order to improve conditions for emigrants.

In this chapter, however, I would like to focus on the lives and work of five Deaf artists—Samuel Close, Sampson Towgood Roch, Lawrence Fagan, Thomas Mahon and Beatrice Gubbins. I choose these five because their lives span two centuries, from the 1740s until the 1940s. These figures also represent different religious and educational traditions among Deaf people in Ireland and demonstrate that both Deaf men and Deaf women have contributed to our artistic and cultural heritage.

Samuel Close (c. 1740–1807)

Samuel Close was born about 1740 and was a native of Dublin. Little is known about his early years or his education but from 1770 until 1780 he carried out a business as an engraver and jeweller at The Ring and Pearl, Upper Blind Quay, in Dublin. He may have known John Duff since they were contemporaries and both lived for a time on Exchange Street. Samuel Close did numerous engravings and illustrations for books and magazines but because of his intemperate habits he earned very little.

He had many plates in *The Hibernian Magazine*, including four small ovals in brown tint, *Morning, Afternoon, Evening* and *Night* which he copied from large coloured pictures. In 1795 he did two views—*The Hot House & Green House at Bellevue* and *Bellevue in the County Wicklow*. He also did many portraits, one of the most important being an oval of General Sir Ralph Abercrombie, who was involved in peace negotiations with the United Irishmen in the 1798 Rebellion. At least fifteen further illustration plates by Samuel Close still survive, two of which are held by the National Gallery.

West View of Merrion-Square.
from the Serpentine Walk, Including Leinster House Clare, &c.

Left: Samuel Close (c. 1740–1807), West View of Merrion Square.
Below: Samuel Close, Evening / Night.

Samuel married Elizabeth Barlow in 1765. One of their sons, also named Samuel, worked for a time as an engraver with his father. Samuel died in 1807 at 134 Capel Street, where he had worked as a hatter since 1785.

Sampson Towgood Roch (1759–1847)

It is likely that both Samuel Close and John Duff knew and conversed with Sampson Towgood Roch, a miniaturist, who, according to the *Dublin Evening Post* of December 18th 1781, had 'removed from Exchange Street to Mr Rice's, 13 Capel Street, where he continues to draw likenesses for bracelets and rings at his usual price of two guineas each.' Roch, who became one of the best known and best paid miniature painters in the 18th century, was born at Woodbine, near Youghal in 1759. Sampson showed an early talent for drawing and on a visit to relatives in Cashel in 1773 he made some sketches of scenery and drew some small portraits of his friends.

 Below: Sampson Towgood Roch (1759–1847), 2 Miniatures.
Right: Lawrence Fagan (1825–1898), Claremont Institution for the Deaf and Dumb.
Right, below: Lawrence Fagan, St. Laurence Gate.
Page 20–21: Lawrence Fagan, Boyne Viaduct, Drogheda

He was sent to Dublin to study but showed little interest and began to paint miniatures instead. By 1784, when he resided at 152 Capel Street, he had gained a name as a miniaturist. In 1786 he left Dublin for Cork and a year later he married his first cousin, Melian Roch, in St Mary's Collegiate Church, Youghal. In 1789 the couple were back in Dublin in Grafton Street where he seems to have been well patronised. Then in 1792 they left for Bath where they remained until 1822. During his stay in England Roch painted several members of the Royal Family as well as naval officers, aristocrats, and numerous wealthy people. He is said to have been offered a knighthood which he declined.

The Roches returned to Ireland in 1822, first to Cork and then to the Roch family home in Co. Waterford. Melian died in 1837 and when Roch himself died ten years later he was buried in the family plot at Ardmore, Co. Waterford. There is no headstone on his grave and the Roches did not have any children. Numerous miniatures by Sampson Roch are in the National Gallery and they are among the best produced by Irish artists. The Holbourne Museum in Bath also holds several miniatures painted by Roch during his time there.

Lawrence Fagan (1825–1898)

Lawrence Fagan was born in the parish of Moore, Listoman, Drogheda, Co. Louth, in 1825. His parents, Sylvester, a poor labourer, and May had

CLAREMONT INSTITUTION FOR THE DEAF AND DUMB.
Engraved by Laurence Feagan, Deaf Mute.

Sketched with a pen by L.F (Deaf Mute)

St LAURENCE GATE.

THE BOYNE V

seven children, and besides Lawrence, there was also a deaf daughter. Unfortunately we know nothing about her, not even her name.

On 28th July 1836 at the age of 11, Lawrence was admitted to the National Institution for the Education of Deaf and Dumb Children of the Poor in Ireland, at Claremont, Glasnevin, which was situated about four miles from the city of Dublin. The National Institution was the first school for the Deaf in Ireland and was founded in 1816. According to the admission book, Lawrence Fagan was pupil number 543. It states that he was born deaf, was quite intelligent and knew some signs. He was taught at Claremont for over six years through the manual alphabet and through sign language probably introduced from the Edinburgh Deaf and Dumb Institution as well from the Birmingham Institution.

Joseph Humphreys, the first trained schoolmaster to work in the National Institution for the Deaf and Dumb, had trained and worked

T ·DROGHEDA.

in both of these institutions. He probably introduced into Claremont the methods of deaf education he had studied at Edinburgh and Birmingham. Under the direction of Humphreys, Lawrence, like the other pupils at Claremont, was instructed in English, arithmetic, art, geography, Irish history and Bible study.

My guess is that Joseph Humphreys was a good art instructor. In fact, he painted a small, greyish water-colour of the Edinburgh Institution and two of the Birmingham Institution which are pasted onto the second page of the first minute book of the National Institution dated about 1818, and which now can be seen in the National Archives, in Bishop Street, Dublin. Among the pupils to whom he taught drawing, engraving, printing and water-colour were Lawrence Fagan, John Johnson and George Naughton.

In 1842 at the age of 17 years, when Lawrence completed his education and was ready to start a career for himself, he left Claremont and settled down in Trinity Street, Drogheda, with his family. He began looking for work there and continued to develop his skills as a draughtsman and sketcher. It is not known whether he worked at home or with an employer. From 1845 he began to draw views of ancient monuments in the locality—round towers, abbeys, monasteries, graveyards, high crosses, churches, tower-gates. He also drew Victorian buildings, street scenes, railway bridges, portraits, hunting scenes, and so on.

We can imagine him as he travelled all over the countryside by horse-drawn cart, occasionally stopping to take out his satchel with pens, ink and paper and his stool and easel to draw his scenes. He was especially fascinated by the archaeological sites of Co. Louth and Co. Meath. He earned a living by selling his works and it is said that he frequented public houses where he would sell his work for drink! This habit, however, does not seem to have affected his ability to work. He was an artist of considerable talent and was very industrious. His work is remarkable for its accuracy and detail. Two of his works, *St Patrick's Cathedral, Dublin* (c.1860) and *Claremont Institution for the Deaf and Dumb*, are now in the National Library of Ireland. Two woodcut prints of *The Thatched Cottages in Santry, Dublin* are in the Municipal Gallery in Dublin.

In 1968, one of Fagan's sketches was sent for restoration work by the owner to a gallery where I happened to be working as a picture framer. When I closely examined the sketch, *Ruins of Monasterboice*, I noticed the tiny lettering, 'by L. Fagan Deaf Mute.' From then on I became preoccupied with finding out more about this Deaf artist. I began my search in the bookshelves of the gallery, starting with two old battered volumes of *A Dictionary of Irish Artists* by Walter G. Strickland, published in 1913. There I found the meagre story of Lawrence Fagan's life and work. After checking in the index I discovered that six other deaf artists were mentioned.

Artists used different kinds of signature for their work, sometimes spelling their names in different ways. Sampson Roch, for example, usually signed and dated his portrait miniatures but his signature varied. Examples survive which are signed 'Roch', 'Roche', 'ROCH', 'S Roche', and 'S. T. Roche', frequently accompanied by a date. Lawrence Fagan usually signed his work, 'drawn by L.F. deaf-mute', 'sketched with pen…

L.F.' and sometimes just 'L. Fagan.' The small print, *Claremont Institution for the Deaf and Dumb*, displays 'engraved by Laurence Fagan, Deaf Mute.' A large pastel portrait of *An Arab Boy in his Costume* is inscribed 'Copied in the Royal Dublin Society by L. Fagan Mute.' This work was presented to the Committee of the Juvenile Deaf and Dumb Association at 28 Molesworth Street where meetings and worship services for Deaf Protestant ex-pupils of Claremont were held.

Seven of Lawrence Fagan's sketches of local scenes in Co. Meath and Co. Louth were shown at the Exhibition of Manufactures, Machinery and Fine Arts held at the Royal Society, Kildare Street, Dublin, in 1864. A large sketch, *Mellifont Abbey,* is part of a private collection in Co. Waterford. I am fortunate to own two of his works, *St. Lawrence Gate, Drogheda* and *Magdalene Tower, Drogheda.* Many of his sketches are probably scattered around the country and hopefully will turn up in the future.

No likeness of Lawrence Fagan himself has been found. It is said that he had red hair and a massive red beard to match and I keep searching in the hope that more examples of his drawings, water-colours or pastels will turn up in the auction rooms, antiques galleries or collection fairs. Lawrence Fagan died a bachelor in 1898 at the age of 73. He is believed to be buried in Drogheda but no trace of his grave has been found.

Thomas Mahon (1864–1939)

Thomas Mahon was born in Baltinglass, Co. Wicklow in 1864. He was Deaf from birth and entered St. Joseph's School, Cabra, in 1871 at the age of seven. According to the school records, Thomas was the 531st pupil admitted to St. Joseph's. He was regarded as an exceptionally intelligent pupil and on the completion of his education his particular abilities for sketching and painting were recognised and encouraged by the school authorities.

In 1880 he attended the studios of an unknown art tutor in Hawkins Street, Dublin, but we have no record of what he learned. In 1884 he accompanied the collector for committee of the Catholic Institution for the Deaf and Dumb, John J. Roe, on a tour of the United States. The purpose of the tour was to raise funds to enable extension work being done in St. Joseph's to continue. Thomas was a gifted artist

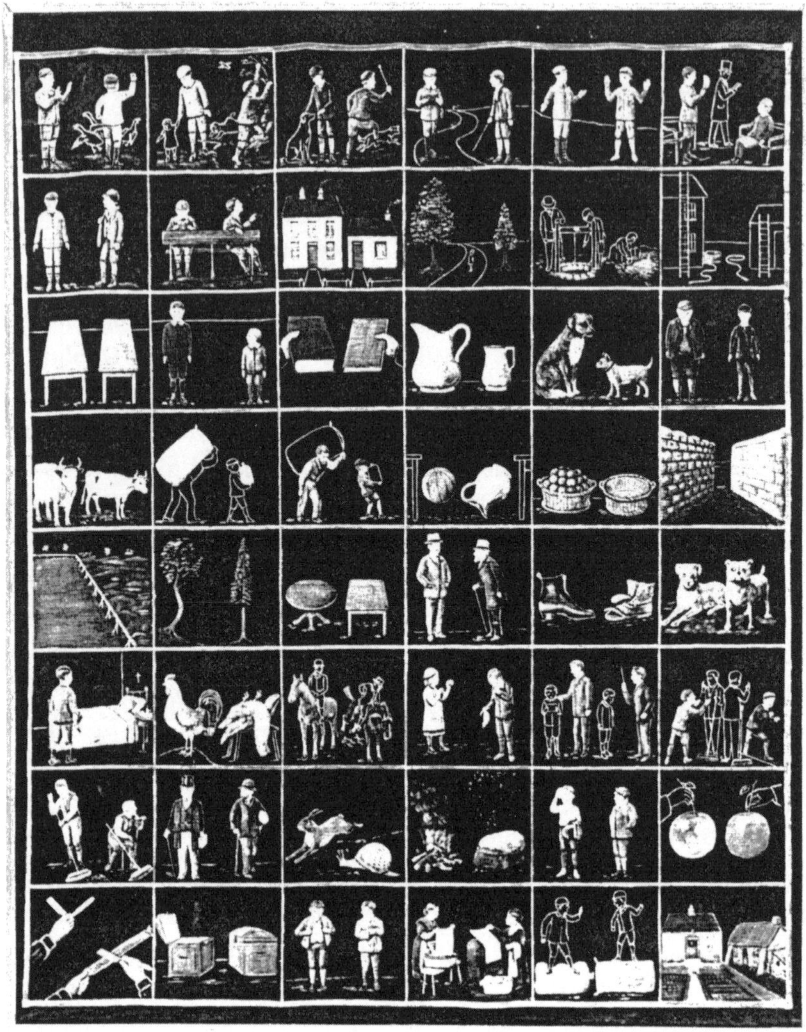

and while Mr. Roe spoke to audiences in the large cities this young Deaf artist astonished those gathered with his quick sketches drawn on a large blackboard: sketches of famous men, animals, scenery and other subjects. The tour was cut short by the death of John Roe and Thomas accompanied the remains back to Dublin. Returning to the States he completed the programme of the tour with another collector. Afterwards he returned alone to Cabra where he was appointed to assist in the educational activities of the school.

Left, and below: Thomas Mahon (1864–1939), untitled.

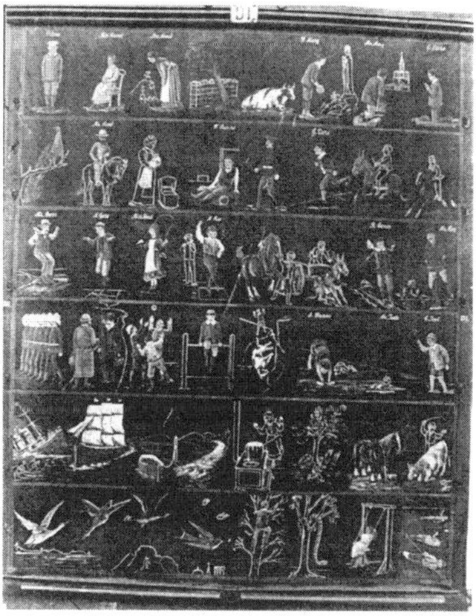

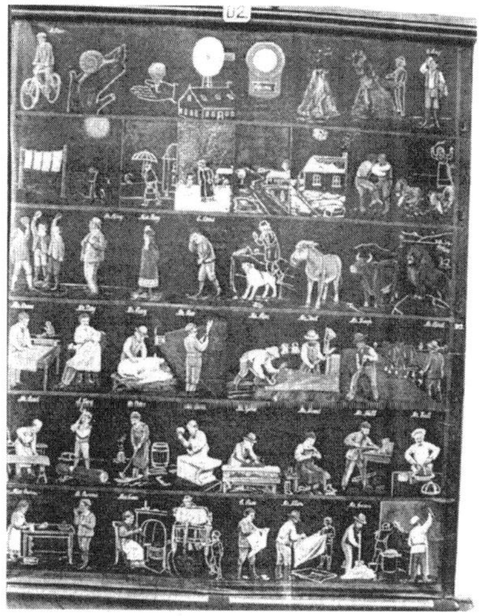

In 1888 he became a full-time teacher of the junior boys, a position which he held for over 45 years. During his time as a teacher he painted up to eighty beautifully executed, instructional charts as part of a graded language course for the school at that time. Thomas got many of his ideas from ancient Egyptian pictograms and signs. The characters of his drawings have a lot in common with hieroglyphics. His experiments with painting hieroglyphic characters worked to his advantage in producing a series of eighty charts containing over six thousand illustrations. These were painted in brilliant colours on a batik black canvas background thus enabling every detail to be easily seen by a class group. Along with objects for vocabulary, the illustrations provided contexts for language structure in the use of verbs, prepositions, adjectives and comparisons, pronouns in their various person and number relationships, possessives, irregular plurals as well as scenes for composition.

Thomas Mahon never married. He died in his tiny, gloomy room in the basement of St. Joseph's in March 1939 at the age of 75 years (he was not a married man) and was buried in the small community cemetery. No headstone was erected on his grave until after World War II, when a number of past-pupils decided to raise the funds to cover the cost

of erecting a handsome headstone. The unveiling ceremony, which took place on 6th August 1954, commemorated a wonderful Irish Deaf painter. Both Deaf and hearing people have been admiring Thomas Mahon's charts for over 90 years. Today a new generations of art lovers can continue to appreciate the Mahon Charts in a new Deaf Heritage Centre at St. Joseph's which opened to visitors in November 2000.

Beatrice Gubbins (1878–1944)

Dunkathel House stands in Glanmire, about three miles outside Cork city. This charming and elegant 18th-century building opened to the public ten years ago. During the 1870s the house was bought by Limerick-born Thomas Wise Gubbins owner of Wise's Distillery on the North Mall. There were seven children in the Gubbins family, five of them girls, all of whom were deaf. More than 50 paintings done by one daughter, Beatrice, are displayed in the exhibition room on the first floor.

Beatrice, the youngest, was born in Limerick in 1878, but lived most of her life at Dunkathel. We have no record of her early education or

Left: Beatrice Gubbins (1878–1944), Landscape.
Above: Beatrice Gubbins, Portrait of a Young Girl.

whether she used sign language but she and her four sisters must have used family signs to communicate with one another. Neither is it clear where she got her early training in art, but she did attend the Crawford School of Art in Cork. The registers there are not extant for the years Beatrice was there but the records show that her sister, Frances Gertrude, was there in 1885.

Beatrice became a talented water-colourist as is evident from the work on display. She was an inveterate traveller and she kept a visual diary of her journeys across Europe and North Africa. As a nurse in World War I she cycled all over Devon sketching and painting. Many of her water colours were done during her various trips. She visited Italy many times and travelled to Morocco in 1929, the West Indies in 1930 and Algeria in 1931.

Beatrice was among the best of the highly talented amateur water colourists working in Ireland during the early part of the twentieth century. Her subject matter was varied and included intimate genre and domestic scenes, still life and landscapes. She exhibited a number of watercolours at the Royal Hibernian Academy in Dublin in 1910 and 1911. For the purpose of anonymity within the highly critical Sketching Club, a local amateur club of which she was secretary, she frequently signed herself 'Greyhound, 'Jessamine' or 'Benjamin.' The collection of her works is one of the main features of the guided tour of Dunkathel. She never married and when she died in 1944 she was was buried in the family plot at Glanmire Church, Cork.

Conclusion

The aim of this chapter has been to record the achievements of a small number of Deaf artists and to highlight their contributions to our heritage. A great deal more research needs to be done and I hope that what is described here will encourage readers to undertake further investigation. Samuel Close, Sampson Twogood Roch, Lawrence Fagan, Thomas Mahon and Beatrice Gubbins faced many difficulties in pursuing their ambitions. Their achievements serve as an example not only for the Irish Deaf community but also for all those who struggle for recognition in Irish society today.

Growing up Deaf in Ireland

Helena Saunders

Introduction

The late 1940s and early 1950s were critical periods in the education of deaf children in Ireland. The first schools for deaf children had been established at the beginning of the nineteenth century. For more than a hundred years signing was the main method of communication, learning and teaching in the classroom. During the late 1940s and early 1950s a very different method of communication and instruction began to be used in the schools. This approach came to be known as oralism. Oralism emphasised speech and speech-reading and the use of microphones and hearing aids. All forms of signing were officially banned both in and outside the classroom. The oral approach was developed by educators who were hearing. Although many had close contact with Deaf communities, their concern was mainly paternalistic. There was no place for Deaf people as teachers, advisers or role models in the oral approach. Many advocates of oralism were also familiar with signing but would not permit it to be used in the classroom. They did not accept that the primary language of the Deaf community, Irish Sign Language, was 'a real language.'

Most accounts of the educational and linguistic experiences of deaf children have been written from the point of view of hearing educators, researchers and administrators. In this chapter I try firstly, to describe, as a Deaf person, my own linguistic experiences during my school years and, secondly, to try to establish a general understanding of the linguistic experiences of children in schools for the deaf in Ireland during the decade 1955–65. This chapter also sets out to present an alternative perspective. It challenges the theory and practice of oralism. Linguistic research has established that sign languages are natural languages, and as such, a sign language constitutes the primary means by which deaf children can learn in school. Any approach that ignores the role of sign language creates major obstacles to the progress and achievement of Deaf students in education. Moreover, individual accounts from Deaf people themselves provide crucial information about what the experience of education was really like. These accounts have been excluded from the oralist perspective.

Since we now know so much about sign languages it is extraordinary that educational institutions have not incorporated this research in their school and teacher training programmes. Andersson (1990a), has deplored the limited knowledge of Deaf people possessed by hearing authors who write on Deaf issues and argues that there is a great need to describe what education was like from the point of view of Deaf people. He proposes that Deaf people should describe their own educational and linguistic experiences. A Deaf perspective gives an alternative account of the education of deaf children, very different from the accounts found in official reports and in texts used in teacher training. It also provides important insights into issues of power and control in education and even into the meaning of deafness.

Deaf or hearing impaired: What does deafness mean?

There are two main discourses on deafness in Irish society today. The dominant discourse is based on an understanding of deafness as a medical or clinical problem. This view understands hearing people to be 'normal' and Deaf people to be 'impaired.' This perspective is expressed in the title and recommendations of the main official document dealing with the education of deaf children in Ireland (The Education of Children who are Handicapped by Impaired Hearing 1972). Deafness is defined only as a matter of being partially or totally unable to hear. Theory and practice in education and in other social services in Ireland have generally accepted this view of deafness. A medical model of deafness assumes that the individual has a 'deficit' or a 'problem.' Great efforts are made to 'cure' or 'fix' Deaf people so that they will be able to 'overcome their problem' and be assimilated into hearing society. In the medical model, all the experts are hearing. Deaf people themselves are usually excluded from significant roles in education and other services (Brien 1992; Lane 1992).

The second discourse regarding deafness has developed more recently. Since the early 1960s studies of sign languages and Deaf communities have changed our understanding of deafness. They have lead to a socio-cultural model of deafness. In this model, the term 'Deaf' has a positive value. A Deaf person does not have a 'deficient' or 'impaired' identity. This model shows that the 'disability' or the 'problem' is not really located in the Deaf individual. The real problems are to be found in the way that society interprets and responds to deafness. According to this socio-cultural model of deafness, for example, low levels of achievement are not attributed to 'hearing impairment.' They are due to social and political issues such as the exclusion of sign language from the schools, inaccessible curricula, unsuitable methods of teaching and the absence of Deaf teachers.

A socio-cultural model of deafness defines sign language and Deaf culture as a normal aspect of human difference. The problems that Deaf people experience are not to be found in their ears but in the structures and responses of society. Deafness is accepted as a normal variation in human diversity. In many recent studies of sign languages and Deaf communities a socio-cultural understanding of deafness is shown by the use of an upper-case 'D' when referring to Deaf people or Deaf communities. When the lower-case 'd' is used it is generally used to refer to a physical impairment and to refer to individuals who are not members of a Deaf community. 'Deaf' refers to a cultural difference and denotes deafness as a cultural trait; 'deaf' refers to an impairment. The first indicates commitment; the second indicates circumstance.

Deaf people have been given many labels, created mostly by the medical profession. Andersson (1990b) states that the creation of new terms or categories, such as 'hearing impaired' or 'prelingually deaf', has brought no advantages to Deaf people and has been adopted mainly for political and administrative purposes. In fact, Deaf people in most countries have rejected the term 'hearing impaired' since it implies that there is something defective about the person. Deaf people regard themselves as members of a distinctive community.

Pre-school experiences

Recently, when I discussed my deafness with my older sister, she told me I never looked up when I was called. My younger sister remembers that my parents thought I was a distant, somewhat heedless child. I can remember that I joined in games with other children. I can also remember that if the game involved turn-taking to a rhyme, such as in skipping games, I found it difficult to know when it was my turn.

There were no such problems with ball games. These games involved matching a sequence of actions using a ball with a sequence of rhyming phrases. For example, the following game involved throwing a ball against a wall:

'One, two, three, (Throw the ball underhand three times)
Over, (Throw the ball once overhand)
Four, five, six, (Three underhand)
Over, (Once overhand)
Seven, eight, nine, (Three times underhand)
Over, (Once overhand)
Ten, (Once underhand)
Over, (Once overhand)
Catch the ball (Three times underhand).'

Before I went to school I did not make any connection—because I was deaf—between the spoken phrase, 'one, two, three,' and the throwing actions but I could carry out all the sets of actions perfectly. I acquired the throwing and catching pattern. Some game patterns were more difficult to learn because the rhyme was connected in a less visible way with the throwing and catching actions. For example: 'Ireland, England, Scotland, Wales, All tied up in donkey's tails.' This game involved throwing the ball as part of a group activity in which each member had to keep pace with the others in the group. The pace was controlled by the oral phrasing which was articulated by another player standing nearby but not throwing the ball. There was another game:

'Flowers in the garden,
Fishes in the sea,
If you want to pick one
Please pick me.'

I developed particular mouth patterns which I used when I played this game. I associated these mouth patterns not with words but with the actions of the game. In fact, it was only when my own children brought the rhymes home from school in children's books that I discovered the words that matched the mouth patterns I had used as a child.

Our family said the Rosary every evening in Irish. In doing so I acquired a sequence of mouth patterns associated with the articulation of the words of the Hail Mary: 'Sé do bheatha Mhuire, tá lán de ghrásta, tá an tiarna leat...' I learned to 'frame' the sequence of words in mouth patterns. By 'frame' I mean that I learned to produce the visual properties of the words but not the vocal properties.

My first school was the local Convent of Mercy primary school. I went for a short time and by the time I left I 'knew' the numbers 1 -10, some prayers, and some vocabulary in Irish, that is, I could recognise and reproduce the visual properties of the words as they appeared when they were articulated. I think that I could speech-read that part of the word that was visual and could reproduce this pattern, or something like it. I could associate what I speech-read and reproduced with the object in question. For example, in Irish the word 'gúna' means 'dress.' Only the vowels 'u' and 'a' are visible on the lips. So what I saw and reproduced was something like 'u-a' and I associated this with the item of clothing worn by girls. So I 'knew' a few individual words, but I had no sentences.

St. Mary's School for Deaf Girls

When I was six years old my mother brought me to the doctor. He probably did the usual tests of hearing—making a quiet noise, speaking behind my back, asking me to carry out some instruction while speaking in a low voice (Whetnall and Fry 1964). The following September I went to St. Mary's School for Deaf Girls in Dublin. My father left my mother and me at the station and when the train pulled out my mother was crying. I am sure she was anxious and worried about me but I had no idea what was happening. A friend of my mother's met us at the station in Dublin and brought us to the school. St. Mary's was a huge building in the suburbs of Dublin. There was another school on the campus, a private school for hearing children, as well as a convent and church.

We went to the parlour and after a while a nun came in. My mother tried to be cheerful and smiling at first but this did not last long. When it was time for her to go, she started to cry. The nun tried to take me away but I would not let go of my mother. Another woman came to help to take me away. I could not stop crying. At first I was put in the infirmary. There were nurses in uniforms and strange smells that made me queasy.

 After a few days I was moved into a large open dormitory. There were two dormitories on the same floor. In one, there were forty beds for the younger pupils and a cubicle for a senior girl. The other dormitory was for the older pupils. Between the two dormitories there was a room for the two nurses.

As time went by, we got used to the routine of travelling back to school after being at home for the holidays. I always had mixed feelings about going back to school. It was hard to leave home but I looked forward to seeing my classmates again. Until we were eleven or twelve years old, every time we came back to school we had to go through a 'cleansing' ritual—a bath, treatment with DDT, and our hair was checked. Our home clothes were put away and we were given our school clothes.

The school day

After we got up at 7.00 am, we walked in twos to Mass in the oratory. Then, at 7.30, we went down to breakfast. From 8.00 to 9.00 we had to do all the tidying, cleaning and polishing chores. We had to make the bed in a particular way. The pillow was put on the top cover. The cover had to be tucked in under the pillow and then pulled over it. The big girls waxed the floors. We younger pupils did the polishing with brushes and cloths. We all had to work in rhythm as we polished. As we worked we had to count 1, 2, 3, 4. The work was supervised and if we broke the rhythm we got a smack with a ruler. Some girls hated this work but I enjoyed it. I liked the rhythmic movement and it kept me warm on cold mornings.

At 9.00 am we assembled in the hall before school. We had to line up in our own class. There were about ten lines, one for each class and one for day pupils. The principal said the prayers and gave out our mail. All the letters were first opened by the school authorities. My mother used to sellotape money on to the letter and put in a bar of chocolate. I got the chocolate but the money was handed over immediately after I had seen it. After the prayers, we filed out to our classrooms and waited outside our classrooms till the teacher arrived. (A few years later we had an account where all the money was put in a press and the amount recorded in a book. There was a sweet-shop then which opened a couple of days in the week.) After the prayers, we filed out to our classrooms and waited outside till the teacher arrived.

Erving Goffman (1968) observed that routine is highly significant in institutions such as residential schools. Our daily lives were dominated by routine. We followed the days of the week by the dinners we ate. We had particular food on particular days of the week—fish on Wednesday and Friday, stew on Monday and Thursday. Goffman also notes the difficulty of finding any privacy in institutions. It was difficult to have any privacy in the school. There was a lot of control over where we could go in the school. We had to go everywhere together—to the classroom, to the refectory, to the oratory, outside for a walk. There was no such thing as arriving late because because we all arrived together. The first time I had to say, 'Sorry I'm late', was when I had left school and was employed by a large retail company. In school some places were out of bounds—the convent, the staff room and the infirmary if we were not sick. There were other spaces which we could use only at appointed times—the refectory at mealtimes, the oratory for Mass, confessions and prayers, the classrooms during school-time. The manual school was particularly out of bounds. Pupils in this school used signs and there was strict segregation between these pupils and 'oral' pupils.

We had a sign that meant 'forbidden' or anything that was not allowed. It consisted of a lip movement articulating something like 'wef.' If you were seen walking by yourself, you were always asked 'Where are you going?' We were not allowed into the kitchen, the laundry or the bakery. There was a great temptation to go into the bakery for bread. If the baker saw us standing there he would get us something. Sometimes, we went in and got it ourselves. If we thought we might be caught we would sign a warning:

Sign: wef '
Gloss: CATCH
Translation: Look out, you will be caught.

Mouthing: wef
handshape: C
location: under the chin without contact
orientation: palm down
movement: quick closing movement of the hand.

The primary school curriculum

I remember that my first class was in the library. A screen separated the class from the glass-fronted book presses. There were twelve pupils in the class. Later we moved into a proper classroom. The table was U-shaped and we all sat around this table. We did not have table microphones or group hearing aids. Other classes had hearing aids which they plugged into the table. In these classes the teacher had a master control on her table which she switched on or off or raised or lowered the volume of the microphones. In our class each pupil had an individual hearing aid—a Medresco. We wore it all the time clipped into our gym-slips. I remember the discomfort of the ear-piece. It was itchy and hot in my ear.

During the early years at school I was in a very mixed class; we were all of different ages, I was the only born-deaf pupil. The others were hard-of-hearing or had become deaf during childhood. Some of my classmates were much older than I: two were adults and others were teenagers. Some of the members of the class had never been to school before. The adult women and older pupils were admitted to the school for basic religious instruction and they left the school soon after they had made their first communion.

Some of the first exercises I remember were picture matching and counting on an abacus. We did drawing and painting. We said prayers at the beginning and end of each period. We said something like, 'Oh Jesus, I love you.' We had no idea what the words meant. The teacher wrote the words on the charts which they hung in the classroom. We imitated as best we could, joining our hands and moving our lips.

Oral education theorists have written of the importance of constructing and maintaining 'an oral environment' (Ewing and Ewing 1964; Calvert and Silverman 1975). Such an oral programme had two aspects. First, speech was to be vigorously promoted. In an oral environment speech was taken to be the primary means of communication. The frequent use of speech was emphasised; everyone—parents, teachers, care staff—were advised to 'talk, talk, talk to the child' (Calvert and Silverman 1975:151). As many opportunities as possible were to be contrived to elicit speech, and pupils were to be continually reminded and encouraged to use speech. The second aspect of oral ideology was to prevent the development of alternative channels of communication among the pupils. If the receivers of a message indicate that they understand non-oral communication pupils will ask themselves, 'Why the use of speech at all' (*ibid* 53).

The curriculum in the primary school in Cabra was organised around an oral methodology. One of the most important influences on the development of oral schooling in Ireland was the Department of Audiology at the University of Manchester. Irene and Alexander Ewing, and later Ethel Ewing, who were the leading figures in the oralist movement in Britain, visited Cabra on a regular basis. They wrote that the primary requisites for a good general education for deaf children were 'speech comprehension, capacity to think in normal language, and learning to talk' (Ewing and Ewing 1964:145). For the Ewings, 'normal' meant spoken, and the complex endeavour of education was reduced to training in speech comprehension and speech production. The basic elements in the curriculum were auditory and sound perception training, and speech training. Of course learning English, reading, writing and numbers were also included in the curriculum but each of these areas was used as the raw material for teaching speech.

Speech teaching was emphasised from our first days at school. The teacher would articulate a word and all together we imitated her. Then we had to articulate each word in pairs. The teacher drew our attention to the sounds that were not visible on the lips—k, t, d, and so on. We were slapped for making mistakes in speech but we were thankful that we were not reported to the principal too often. Speech training permeated all aspects of the curriculum. For example, a lot of work went into preparation for oral confession. We had to learn the appropriate words of the prayer. We also had to practise 'saying our sins':

> I talked in class.
> I disobeyed the teacher.
> I signed in the dormitory.
> I did not pay attention at Mass.
> I did not say my prayers.
> I told a lie.

We drew up a full list of potential sins. Then, from this list, we wrote down our own private list of sins. When we had learned it off by heart we tore it up. Then we went to the oratory and we all said our prayers before confession. Each one of us made her confession orally. When we had finished we said the prayers after confessions and then the penance of three Hail Marys together.

Speech development continued to be an important part of the curriculum during our senior years in the primary school. At this stage, speech practice was usually based on a poem:

> Slowly, silently now the moon
> Walks the night in her silver shoon
> This way and that she peers and sees
> Silver fruit upon silver trees.

Underlining the letters and adding numbers were used to draw our attention to the sound, syllable and stress patterns:

1 2	1 2 3	1 2	1	1 2
Slow-ly,	si-lent-ly	n-ow	the	moo-n

Some sounds were considered to be very important. Our attention was continually drawn to these sounds. The important sounds were s, t, k, n, m, d, ing. These sounds were always underlined by the teacher. There was a system of hand movements and positions around the face which were associated with the articulation of specific sounds. It is ironic that a system of signs was used to teach better articulation skills:

a, o	hand on chest
e	hand under the chin
b, p	hand in front of lips
k, g, c	little finger points to open mouth
sh	index finger in front of lips
m	hand on side of face
n	index finger on nose
ing	index finger on nose and little finger points to open mouth
ch	thumb forward from mouth
c, s	hand in front of the lips or use of a feather
r, t	particular movement of index finger in front of the mouth
f	hand in front of the lips and feel the air

We practised making these sounds over and over again, but the use of speech in a natural context did not arise for us. There were few opportunities to use these exercises as part of an interaction in spoken language with hearing persons outside class. We did not see any connection between what we were doing in class and having a conversation in speech with a hearing person in the world outside the classroom. When the teachers told us that our speech was 'good' we believed them. We thought it would be possible for us to interact comfortably with the hearing world through speech. When I tried to talk at home no one could understand me.

We practised speech-reading by dictation. The teacher usually used extracts from our written work. The teacher said a sentence and we had to write it down. We often had to guess particular words because the articulation of some words gave us no visible clues. For example, we never knew whether it was 'had' or 'has.'

Much of our learning was by rote. In our catechism lessons we learned to list off the seven deadly sins—Pride, Covetousness, Lust, Anger… We did not know the meaning of any of these words. In fact I only discovered what they meant when I left school. I remember that I disliked the word 'lust' in particular because of the very difficult 'st' combination and 'covetousness' because the syllables were easily forgotten. Catechism was another opportunity for practising speech without bothering too much about the meaning of what we were learning.

The school kept a very close supervision over our hearing aids. They had to be worn at all times. The teacher checked them every morning to make sure they were in working order and we were expected to report any fault first thing in the morning in class. If we did not report, we were scolded. We did not dare not to wear it. It was uncomfortable at times and was never allowed to be covered by our cardigans. Wearing hearing aids became a habit. Ewing and Ewing (1964:26) recommended that 'every hearing impaired child needs to have his hearing re-tested and re-assessed at least once each year.' At least once a year our hearing was assessed and new ear moulds were made. A lot of time was wasted checking, testing and fitting and so on. It was all part of the ritual of oralism.

From the middle of the 1950s, auditory learning was an important part of the curriculum. The pupils were trained to distinguish between different kinds of sounds—between loud and quiet, between high and low, between sounds with fast rhythm and sounds with a slow rhythm. There was a special stage in the play-hall which was equipped with an organ and two powerful loudspeakers. The theory was that training in sound awareness would help our speech. After some time the programme was linked to auditory training and movement with different kinds of rhythms. That was the theory but in practice it did not work like that for the students. In my experience there was no direct link between the awareness of sounds and rhythmic movement. When we moved we counted time—march-time, waltz-time and Irish dancing-time. When we moved we depended on our counting, not on the sounds of the music. Movement to music helped us 'to move gracefully' and 'to breathe properly' (McIllroy 1996). It kept us fit and occupied. But there was very little link between that and speech.

Teaching and learning English

In the first stages of language teaching there was a lot of emphasis on building up a basic English vocabulary. It was obvious if we were to make progress in spoken language we had to know the words for things (Ewing and Ewing 1964:47). The teachers used charts, pictures, cards, and written words. We had a list of farm animals, clothes, furniture, colours, food and so on. As we got older we were introduced to a particular system for learning English sentence patterns. Every day the teacher wrote 'The News' on the board:

> Today is…
> Yesterday was…
> Tomorrow will be…
> It is the…(date)
> It is…(weather)
> Today is the feast of…(particulars of the day).

Then other appropriate or topical sentences were included:

> We went for a walk to the farm yesterday.
> Mary got a letter from home.
> We will have pancakes tomorrow.

These sentences were first elicited from the pupils. As the correct answers were given they were written on the blackboard. We then copied the sentences into our copybooks. We read the news from the board while the teacher corrected our speech as we read aloud.

Teaching English structures, especially word order, became more important during my final years in the primary school. Teachers used a number system as a framework for these language lessons. The following examples show how the system worked:

```
(1)   1    2 0 3
      John is a boy
(2)   0  1          2  5
      The blackboard is black
```

Each part of speech was assigned a number 0—6. A typical lesson proceeded as follows: the teacher wrote a sentence on the board. The pupils were then asked to identify the parts of speech in the sentence. When we said 'noun' the teacher wrote 1 over the appropriate word. We would complete several sentences in this way. Ordinarily the match between each number and part of speech could be made in a straightforward way. Occasionally, certain mysterious combinations occurred which puzzled us. For example:

```
(3)   1      1
      Mary's jumper
```

It was difficult to accept that two number 1s could occur together. Why wasn't the second word a 2 or a 3?

```
(4)   0  1          2  5
      The blackboard is black.
```

We could not understand why 'black' was not an object (3). After all the 1, 2, 3 sequence was very common. Why should 'black' be a 5? There were other symbols for changes in the form of the verb. The present tense was indicated by a 2, the past tense was indicated with a leftward arrow over the 2 and the future with a rightward arrow over the 2.

It is probably true to say that we never made any real connection between 'ed' and its temporal meaning. Similarly at this stage I did not grasp the difference between 'a' and 'the' or between 'was' and 'were' or between 'had, 'has' and 'have.' The system was based on developing the receptive form of English. There was much less time given to teaching productive English. We never had to make our own sentences and put in the numbers.

Communication among pupils

Halliday (1975) argues that when children are developing language skills they are learning how to express meaning. Learning how to mean was not part of our classroom experience in language learning. When we were practising speech we were learning how to articulate; we were not learning to mean. Of course we had to develop other ways to express meaning. We had to develop an alternative system. For us, learning to mean grew out of our need to communicate with one another.

As I remember it, as children we gradually developed a system of communication among ourselves. We built our linguistic system by borrowing from the world we lived in, from home and from the world of the school. During my early years we had no access to signing adults. There were no children who had deaf parents from whom we could acquire a sign language. The children, who began as oral pupils, were segregated from the older children who had been taught under the manual system. We never really had access to any signing models. We created sign names for teachers out of familiar characteristics—an unusual walk, a particular hairstyle or kind of make-up, the shapes of the glasses they wore, or how they administered punishment (tugging an ear, rapping knuckles). We borrowed the actions and movements of the people around us at school and at home and these became the raw materials for the development of a language for our own pupil-based community.

Goldin-Meadow (1977) and Feldman, Goldin-Meadow and Gleitman (1978) report on the development of signing among children who did not have access to signing models. These studies suggest that deaf children can begin to develop a sign language in the absence of adult models. Goldin-Meadow reported the emergence of two-sign utterances. Feldman *et al* found that the children in their study developed substantial lexicons of invented signs. They also reported that the children's utterances were governed by basic grammatical rules, for example, when an actor was specified in an utterance it occurred in the first position.

Mohay (1982) reported the development of two-sign utterances in the absence of adult signing models. However, she concluded that the communication systems generated by the children, at the point at which the research was carried out, did not appear to constitute a true linguistic system. Despite these limitations, the children were able to express all of the semantic functions found in the early stages of language development. Thus, according to Mohay's study, language development occurs but is delayed in the absence of language models.

Volterra (1983) has criticised these findings. In a study of the development of gestures, she compared the hearing children of hearing parents with a Deaf child of Deaf parents. All the children in her study developed gestures that named objects or actions, such as DRINK and TELEPHONE (referential gestures). They also developed deictic gestures by pointing or reaching to objects and locations (for example, THIS and THERE). All the children progressed to combinations of two deictic gestures (THAT THERE) and of a deictic and a referential gesture (THAT DRINK). However, only the Deaf child, who was exposed to an adult model of sign language developed combinations of two referential gestures (FISH EAT).

Volterra re-analysed the Goldin-Meadow data in the following way: deictic, referential, deictic+deictic, deictic+referential, and referential+referential. She claims that none of the children in Goldin-Meadow's study combine two referential gestures. She goes on to argue that the capacity to combine two referential symbols indicates the emergence of a true linguistic system and that such development depends on access to a language model.

My own school experience, at least in the early stages, does not seem to substantiate Volterra's argument. I do not remember that we had access to any sign language models, either signing adults or pupils who had Deaf parents. I do remember that we developed an extensive lexicon in sign, based, as I have observed, on actions, objects and states taken from the world around us. An example was SATURDAY (wash hair). This sign was derived from the fact that our hair was washed every Saturday. We combined referential signs: CAKE BE-AWFUL (the cake is awful), MARY SICK + hand on forehead (Mary is sick), and TWO TWO (get into twos).

In ordinary circumstances, the acquisition of language and the progression from one stage of development to another is a complex process. The complexity greatly increases when access to adult language models is absent, when transmission occurs through the child population, and when a difference between language modes (sign and speech) cuts across the acquisition process. A great deal of further linguistic research is required among the deaf school-going population. Such research will enable us to get a clearer picture of the manner in which deaf children of hearing parents acquire sign language, of the stages in this process, and of how the variety of language used in the schools compares with adult usage. Research of this kind is of particular importance since so many deaf children of hearing parents now attend mainstream schools where there are no signing models and the numbers of deaf children may be too small to constitute a viable signing community.

Many researchers have observed that even in a highly controlled and strictly supervised oral environment, deaf children use movement and action to create and express meaning. Oralist theory stressed that the oral programme had to be extended beyond the classroom and the care staff were expected to enforce oral communication among the pupils (Calvert and Silverman 1975:52). At mealtimes and playtimes we were not supposed to sign to one another. Signing was strictly forbidden. The teachers emphasised that signing was 'very stupid, that if we signed we would 'never learn' and 'never be able to talk.'

If we were caught signing we were punished in a variety of ways e.g. slapped, deprive of treats like sweets and cakes (Burns 1995:159). We were put out on the classroom corridor, were picked on, and told, 'You are very stupid. You are always signing. Go to the back of the queue.' The principal slapped pupils who were sent to her for signing. Most of the corporal punishment administered in the school was administered for signing. Speech was connected to moral behaviour; signing was related to disobedience and sin.

We had to communicate, so when we signed among ourselves we always had to keep a watch out for 'nurses', 'nuns' or 'teachers.'

> The pupils were under constant surveillance and since the staff was outnumbered, older pupils were encouraged to report incidents of signing to the school authorities. We were

> not really afraid of the older pupils. They might tell us to stop signing but they didn't report us. Anyway they themselves signed too. (McDonnell and Saunders 1993:257)

I remember there was one pupil who was the 'storyteller.' We would all gather around her when she had a story to narrate. She had to keep a watch out for the care staff. If anyone came along she stopped signing and pretended to 'talk.' She told stories about the films that she had seen. She had marvellous descriptive powers, detailing the expressions of the actors, how they walked, their clothes and houses, the love scenes. We learned a lot from her; we understood her stories but of course we had no English words for the signs.

Nevertheless, the strategies against signing had a powerful effect on our attitudes, values and beliefs (*ibid* 1993). As pupils we were very aware of the 'forbidden' nature of signing. Even though we developed strategies to circumvent the ban on signing we felt guilty and bold for doing so. We believed what we were told. We believed that signing was bad, stupid and dangerous. Of course, we could not stop because we had to communicate. When we tried to use speech we could not understand one another. We did not know how English worked.

During the last year in primary school we had a group hearing aid system. The teacher had a microphone. The sound was relayed to each pupil at the U-shaped table. We had to plug our headphones into a socket in the table and adjust the volume ourselves. This system produced background noise but did not improve our capacity to discriminate between speech sounds. I could distinguish the teacher's voice and my own voice but only as a kind of background noise. During this year I noticed that more and more visitors were coming into the class. Perhaps it was due to the fact that our class now had a group hearing aid system. This was a new occurrence that broke the monotony of school. The visitors were mostly male. We thought they were doctors because of their white coats. The change helped to develop our communication and signing skills since we now had something to comment on and make remarks about. Pupils were selected to give prepared answers: What is your name? Where are you from? A warning was given not to sign.

The post-primary curriculum

The secondary department in the school was quite small. At this time second level education for deaf girls was a new idea. Around this time, the early 1960s, deaf girls began to sit for public examination for the first time. In 1959, two students did the matriculation examinations—an entrance examination for university (Buckley 1997). At this time Irish was a compulsory subject at second level. However, exemption from Irish in matriculation had been granted to the school in 1958 by University College, Dublin. A similar exemption was extended to the Intermediate and Leaving Certificate examinations. In 1963, five girls sat for the Intermediate Certificate examination in six subjects—Latin, English Language, History and Geography, Elementary Mathematics, Domestic Science and Drawing.

There was less emphasis on speech in the secondary department. I think there was no time because so many other subject areas had to be covered. Most of our efforts involved reading, writing, and speech-reading. There was no time for spoken language. I did not feel any loss. I felt I was learning. There was new information and knowledge to be acquired. The teaching was more flexible. When I had finished one lesson I was free to move on to the next. As a result my learning experiences at second level were much more positive than in the primary school.

Although we had text books most of the resources and class materials were developed by the teachers themselves. The lessons in history for example were prepared by the teacher in a simplified format that we had to copy out and learn off by heart. When we wrote English essays the teacher corrected them and used the corrections to illustrate and teach English structure and word order. I used to read my hearing sisters' English books and do grammar exercises from them. Signing was forbidden at second level but the supervision was not as strict as in primary school. We always signed with one another when the teacher's back was turned. But at the back of my mind there was always the notion that signing would affect my cognitive development in a negative way.

After doing well in the Intermediate Certificate Examination, when I came back to school in September I expected to enter the Leaving Certificate class. However, I was then told that I would not be allowed to study for the Leaving Certificate. It seemed that this decision was made after an assessment by the school psychologist. I was given no explanation. Although one of my teachers appealed to the principal and offered to support me during my studies the decision was not changed. When I asked the teacher for an explanation, he said it was because I was 'profoundly deaf.' I believe there was a much more positive attitude regarding the prospects of partially deaf and deafened students than the prospects of deaf students. For the reminder of the year I was put in as a classroom assistant in the manual school and asked to supervise infants at playtimes. The following July I started a three-month diploma course as Comptometer Operator and in October I received the diploma standard of competency.

Conclusion

It was not until I was six years old and had a hearing test that I was sent to St. Mary's School for Deaf Girls. Prior to this I learned to 'frame' a sequence of words in mouth patterns. I learned to reproduce the visual properties of the words. This continued to be an important part of my experience of spoken language during my school life and into my adult life. St. Mary's set out to construct and maintain an oral environment. It permeated all aspects of the curriculum and was the focus of all classes. The meaning of words was not as important as the ability to say them. By saying or attempting to say them we were wrongly led to believe our speech could be understood by the hearing world.

As pupils whose primary need was to communicate with one another, we gradually acquired a sign language. We constructed our linguistic system by borrowing from the visual world we lived in. I do not remember that during my early school years we had access to adult signing models. However, we did develop a lexicon and syntax in sign and by the time we entered secondary school we were signers within our own school community. In secondary school, while signing was still unacceptable, it was more widely used and the emphasis on speech in the classroom lessened. Words took on meanings and the curriculum a life. This life, for me, was short-lived as I was not allowed to do the Leaving Certificate apparently for no other reason except that I was profoundly deaf.

References

Andersson, Y. (1990a) Who should make decisions on communication among Deaf people? in *Deaf American*, Washington DC: National Association of the Deaf.

Andersson, Y. (1990b) The Deaf world as a linguistic minority, in S. Prillwitz and T. Vollhaber (eds) *Sign Language Research and Application, International Studies on Sign Language and Communication of the Deaf, Volume 13*, Hamburg: Signum-Press.

Brien, D. (ed.) (1992) *Dictionary of British Sign Language / English*, London: Faber and Faber.

Buckley, M. (1997) Personal communication, 2nd September.

Burns, S. (1995) *Irish Sign Language as a Minority Language*, unpublished dissertation, Centre for Language and Communication Studies, University of Dublin, Trinity College.

Calvert, D. and Silverman, S. (1975) *Speech and Deafness*, Washington DC: Alexander Graham Bell Association.

Department of Education (1972) *The Education of Children Who Are Handicapped by Impaired Hearing*, Dublin: The Stationery Office.

Ewing A. and Ewing, E. (1964) *Teaching Deaf Children to Talk*, Manchester: University of Manchester Press.

Feldman, H. Goldin-Meadow, S. and Gleitman, L. (1978) Beyond Herodotus: The creation of language by linguistically deprived children, in A. Lock (ed.) *Action, Gesture and Symbol: The Emergence of Language*, London: Academic Press.

Goffman, E. (1968) *Asylums: Essays on the Social Situation of Mental Patients and Other Inmates*, Harmondsworth: Pelican Books.

Goldin-Meadow, S. (1977) Structure in a manual communication system developed without a conventional language model: Language without a helping hand, in H. Whitaker and H. A. Whitaker (eds) *Studies in Neurolinguistics 4*, New York: Academic Press.

Halliday, M. (1975) *Learning How to Mean*, London: Edward Arnold.

McIllroy, R. (1996) Auditory training and dance, in T. Broderick and R. Duggan (eds) *St. Mary's School for Deaf Girls 1846–1996*, Dominican Convent, Cabra, Dublin.

Lane, H. (1992) *The Mask of Benevolence*, New York: Random House.

McDonnell, P. and Saunders, H. (1993) Sit on your hands: Strategies to prevent signing, in R. Fischer and H. Lane (eds) *Looking Back: A Reader on the History of Deaf Communities and their Sign Languages*, Hamburg: Signum-Press.

Mohay, H. (1982) A preliminary description of the communication systems evolved by two deaf children in the absence of a sign language model, *Sign Language Studies*, 34: 73–90, The Hague: Mouton Publishers.

Volterra, V. (1983) Gestures, signs and words at two years, in J. Kyle and B. Woll (eds) *Language in Sign: An International Perspective on Sign Languge*, London: Croom Helm.

Whetnall, E. and Fry, D. (1964) *The Deaf Child*, London: The Whitefriars Press.

Deaf students' views on access to public examinations at Second Level

Carmel Grehan

Introduction

In Ireland students in post primary education sit for two major public examinations. The Junior Certificate examination is taken at the end of the Junior Cycle which represents the first three years of post primary education. The Junior Certificate was introduced in 1989 to replace the Intermediate Certificate[1] and Day Vocational (or Group) Certificate[2] programmes. The Leaving Certificate programme represents the final two years of post primary education and is offered in two main forms—Leaving Certificate and Leaving Certificate Applied. The Leaving Certificate is seen as a highly academic programme and is taken by the great majority of students. The Leaving Certificate Applied was introduced in 1997 and is strongly oriented to vocational education. None of the interviewees in the research discussed in this paper sat for the Leaving Certificate Applied.

The main schools for Deaf pupils in Ireland, St Mary's for girls and St. Joseph's for boys, were first officially recognised as special national schools by the Department of Education in 1952 (The Education of Children Who Are Handicapped by Impaired Hearing 1972:173). Post primary courses were introduced in 1954 at St. Mary's and in 1964 at St. Joseph's, although students taking these courses did not sit for any public examination. The first Deaf students to sit for a public examination were two Deaf girls who sat the Matriculation examination for entry into University College Dublin in 1959. The first Deaf students to sit for the Intermediate Examination did so in St. Mary's in 1963, and in 1971 the first Deaf girl from St Mary's sat for the Leaving Certificate.

In 1967, three Deaf boys from St. Joseph's sat for the Group Certificate examination and by 1969/70 thirty-six Deaf boys were following Intermediate or Group Certificate courses. Deaf boys in St. Joseph's first sat for the Leaving Certificate in 1980.

The views of the participants

The purpose of the research discussed here is to investigate the experiences of Deaf students in post primary education as they prepared and sat for public examinations. Eight former students were interviewed, four of whom sat for the Leaving Certificate between 1997 and 2000 and four who sat for examinations in or before 1980. The background details of the participants are outlined in Table 1. All the participants attended either St. Mary's or St. Joseph's Schools for the Deaf in Cabra. One of the younger female participants left the Deaf school at the age of 15 and attended a mainstream school until she left at age of 18.

TABLE 1: BACKGROUND EDUCATION OF THE PARTICIPANTS

ID	Sex	Left school	Aged	Certificate examination
Younger respondents				
1	M	1997	20	Leaving
2	M	2000	19	Leaving
3	F	1997	20	Leaving
4	F	1998	18	Leaving
Older respondents				
5	M	1973	16	Group
6	M	1980	20	Leaving
7	F	1978	16	Intermediate
8	F	1973	17	Intermediate

The average age for sitting Leaving Certificate examinations in the younger group was 19:3. In the older group the average age for sitting the Intermediate Certificate examinations was 17:3, after which the pupils left school. The range of subjects taken for the various examinations is listed in Table 2. All participants took English and Mathematics as core subjects. In the British education system, Science is one of the core subjects. This is not so in Ireland. None of the interviewees had studied a modern European language. Males took technical subjects such as Technical Drawing while females took Home Economics.

TABLE 2: SUBJECTS TAKEN FOR EXAMINATION

Male	Female
Younger respondents (for Leaving Certificate)	
Art	Art
Construction Studies	Business Organisation
English	English
Geography	Geography
Link Module (LCVP)	History
Maths	Home Economics
Technical Drawing	Maths
Older respondents	
(for Group Certificate)	(for Inter Certificate)
English	Art
Geography	English
History	History and Geography
Maths	Home Economics
Mechanical Drawing	Latin
Woodwork	Maths
(for Leaving Certificate)	Science
Art	
Biology	
Building Construction	
Technical Drawing	

Almost all participants said they prepared for their examinations. The younger group prepared by practising with previous examination papers. According to one younger male student, some teachers arranged extra hours for class work after school to prepare for examinations. One of the younger female students had a private tutor at home. Another younger female had free periods in her timetable due to exemption from Irish and stated that her teacher revised all the subjects and provided notes, which were very helpful. In the older group, the females could not say clearly if they had prepared beforehand. For example:

> 'I studied by heart—I thought I did prepare but my poor results meant that I didn't prepare.'

and

> 'I did well in my examinations so I must have studied well.'

According to an older male respondent, football from 3–5 pm was cancelled by the school for two weeks before the examinations began. There was an extra hour given for study after tea break and the boys studied under a supervisor. Another older male (a day pupil) stated that his parents were very strict and instructed him to study every weekend. It became a habit for him to be organised in his preparations. So it seemed that the teachers had prepared them rather than the students preparing themselves.

All the older participants reported that they felt nervous on the day of the examination. Three younger participants said they had mixed feelings and wanted it to be over as quickly as possible. One young female student said she felt calm. Almost all had similar experiences in their lack of understanding of the examination questions. Difficulties arose because English was not their first language. As one young male explained:

> 'The English paper (Paper 2) was difficult because of the grammar/language. I had to re-read it through to make myself understand. Also for Mathematics, Paper 2 was difficult with lots of English language in it.'

However one participant was well prepared:

> 'I had practised twenty years' previous examination papers. The first few years were hard but then it become easier because questions were easier to read. I was well prepared with similar questions from old examination papers. I went to the Institute of Education during mid-term break and also at weekends, practising how to answer the questions.'

She went on to say:

> 'If St. Mary's provided a good education and good teaching we would have understood the questions. The reason I left was because I was not learning new vocabulary... Teachers omitted words that they thought the Deaf didn't need to learn but I learned more new words in the mainstream school. When Deaf students read the questions, they don't know what it means. Why? Because they lack the vocabulary.'

Normally, no help was allowed but with English as their second language, reading examination papers was difficult for the students. Only two male students received help because their teachers came into the examination room. Teachers were aware of the regulations but maybe they had a habit of 'spoonfeeding' pupils, so pupils were dependent on them. An older male participant illustrates:

> 'My teacher was allowed to enter the examination room. The superintendent from outside was there. I didn't understand something, so my teacher came to me, and explained in sign language. Also in English, I didn't understand but he explained that I didn't have to do all the questions, just pick what I was asked. I was relieved. Without the teacher's explanation, I would have felt lost.'

On the other hand, an older female respondent had a different experience in her English examination:

> 'The exam paper offered a choice from sections A or B or C. I did one from each and then after the exams, I asked other girls and they had done the same. I was relieved because I was not sure at first then when the teacher asked us how we got on, I explained. He was furious and said we should have picked A or B or C, not a question from each of these sections. But strangely we passed the exams. I didn't know how. He didn't explain or prepare for exams. Now they have sample papers; we didn't have them.'

So who was at fault? Should the teachers take responsibility to explain clearly about the choice of questions beforehand? Some participants seemed to blame teachers for not preparing them. According to the same female quoted immediately above: 'We had a very bad English teacher.' Another older male recalled that during the Woodwork examinations, one boy was very upset so the teacher helped to fix his work for him and he got an A for it. However, it is a puzzle that the older group reported that they had never been provided with or practised on sample papers.

As we have seen, participants were struggling with their examinations. So the next question was whether they were able to concentrate on their work or whether their attention wandered. Unlike the older group, most of the younger interviewees reported being able to concentrate. The younger group may have been more focused than the older group because they had practised on past papers and were better able to attempt the questions. It is significant that one older male who had practised on past papers reported being able to concentrate on the examination. He had taken a pre-examination course with hearing students for four days and was provided with papers from previous examinations:

> 'I tried not to look at others. One time I looked at one boy, he smiled at me, made my confidence low. Thinking that he had no problem with his exams I had to concentrate myself.'

An older male who said it depended on how good he was at the subjects:

> 'On some subjects I was good at concentrating, but in Woodwork I was hopeless so I remember looking at other boys because I was weak in that area... I was doing poorly and others were doing well. That made me more nervous.'

An older female reported:

> 'I didn't think about it until the hearing students finished earlier and left. They were outside chatting. I looked at them through the window, thinking they were lucky to be finished and I felt I was behind.'

It seems that mixing with hearing pupils in the examination may make Deaf candidates feel more nervous because hearing pupils may have more confidence in English writing. Another older female was not concentrating because she was worried about her English grammar:

> 'Most hearing students looked confident and carried on writing. I was stuck, didn't know the answers or how to write correctly. I spent time worrying about grammar.'

Interviewees were asked if they had enough time to complete their answers. All the younger group said they had enough time because the new regulations for candidates with a disability allows additional time (Ten minutes extra in a one hour exam). In the younger group, two interviewees said that they needed more time for Mathematics even though they were allowed an extra ten minutes. English grammar was mentioned again:

> 'I didn't have enough time…As I said I used up a lot of time trying to understand the questions. I worried about the grammar in the English examination, and also with other subjects. English is my second language.'

Most interviewees were relieved and happy when the examinations were over. All the female interviewees discussed the examination with others afterwards while only two of the males did so. Generally, all except one participant were happy with their results. Looking at what they said in more detail, one female remembered how upset she was when she failed English:

> 'I failed English and passed other subjects. But failing English, I felt that I failed all. I was very upset.'

In a paper that combined History and Geography, another older female participant failed History. She stated that History was her weak area so she didn't bother studying:

> 'I was not surprised, as I knew that I didn't do well but I passed Geography. It helped.'

English is a major problem, one older male said:

> 'The comprehension is a problem, a question can be like a word game as it can be based on sound. Hearing people can get the idea by hearing but for Deaf people it is off the point.'

This leads to limited choice:

> 'In English class, I learned three sections—Play, Novel and Poem. They were important areas in the examination... There were two choices in each section, for example, the play 'Playboy of the Western World' and 'Hamlet' and also another two sections for the novel. I didn't have any choice, just focused on the 'Playboy of the Western World' because it was only one that I studied in the class...Then after the examination, I found that the 'Hamlet' questions were easier. I wished I had the same information as the hearing students. They had choices, I had none.'

In conclusion, there were no significant differences between the two groups in preparing for the examinations but the younger group seemed to have more confidence than the older group. They had similar problems in English language and they struggled to understand the questions. It should be noted that English and Mathematics kept being mentioned by the participants, especially English, and more so in the older group. Overall, during the examinations, they spent time worrying over English language and took more time to understand the questions. It seems likely that using sign language in the examinations would be supportive.

Looking back

Interviewees were asked if ISL (Irish Sign Language) should be used in public examinations. Surprisingly, three out of the eight interviewees did not support the use of ISL. One stated:

> 'It's hard to say because I was brought up in an oral school and got used to it. Maybe if I failed, I would have, but I passed my exams so I don't know.'

A younger female interviewee was not sure about it because she believed that English language is important:

> 'It's hard to say—because it is more difficult to sign in video if the subject is Mathematics. If everyone had their own way, they would want oral exams. If we used sign in English exams,

fine, but we would leave out lots of words.'

An older male doesn't support it because he believes in equality with hearing people in order to live in the same society:

> 'No, I don't believe it. It means that I am a special case, treated differently from the hearing and we live in the world of reading/literature…Equal rights in one area then disability treatment in other area, it doesn't make sense to me.'

If ISL was permitted in exams would participants have preferred 'live' interpretation of the questions or a prepared video tape? More interviewees thought they would have preferred a video tape even though:

> 'With interpreters you can ask for clarification while with video you can't ask for clarification.'

and

> 'Live interpretation would be more comfortable, video is more artificial. I never tried it but if I used both I could tell the difference. But I can imagine using an interpreter is more comfortable.'

Three of the participants had different views. One said:

> 'I could watch the video repeatedly. If I was using an interpreter, it would be difficult to ask for a repeat; others might not want a repeat but with the video it can be done in the student's own time…other students would not lose time.'

One older male had a different view about using either interpretation or a video tape. Again he wanted to have the same conditions as hearing people have:

> 'I would see what the hearing world had. Do they have real life voice translating? They don't, they have exam papers on a table. So I think it should be the same for the Deaf. But if I had to choose I'd choose video because the video tape is like a paper, it can't be changed.'

Only one female didn't support either video or interpreting, stating:

> 'No, why should we be different…'

There was then a question of whether they would have liked to use sign language in answering questions in the examination. Surprisingly, three older and one of the younger interviewees did not support the use of sign language in answering examination questions because they believed in the importance of English. An older male participant said:

> 'I was glad that I was forced to write. It means that I can be prepared for a hearing university…Gallaudet [University]… highly recommend English writing. I don't want to be a black sheep of society. I believe writing is very important. If we can't write, society's attitude would be negative to us, calling us lazy.'

He went on to say:

> 'If others have been damaged by the system in education in their lives, they should be allowed to use video but I wouldn't allow video use to have a negative influence on writing skills in the future…I mean that even if Deaf students are allowed to use ISL in future examinations students who grow up through a good system of education should still be able to write.'

An older female agreed:

> 'I want to prove to myself that I can use writing to access the world. It's hard to explain but I don't want to tell you that I think using video in ISL is no good…Yes, video is important for those who have received a poor education and have no English. They can use the video but for those who grow up with good written English, they can write. It is good practice for being in the hearing world, looking for a job, writing in every day life. If I had poor English, I would use video but I am good, so I chose writing.'

So interviewees believe that English is very important and only support ISL if Deaf students had received a poor education. There was some confusion among interviewees as to what was being measured in examinations. One stated:

> 'First, ISL users should have access but if I use ISL how can I measure my English skills, how can I recognise good English skills?...Maybe a bilingual approach—first use ISL then write to show English skills...If I ignore written English, how can I communicate in future every day life in the hearing world by writing or faxing? I can't have 24 hours interpreting and I need confidence to write. My English is average but I can write in every situation. I think writing is very important. I think [examination candidates] should be given choices, first to answer in ISL and then to answer in writing.'

Two people thought ISL would be a better option:

> 'Writing in English gives limited access...if [candidates] use ISL, they can give more information and won't be limited.'

and

> 'If I write in English, the marker might think I meant something different to what I wanted to answer so my answer would look wrong. In ISL I could give a clear answer.'

One older female said she didn't know whether she would have wanted to use ISL in her examinations because she had never had that particular experience. But she was aware that when she wrote, she worried about English grammar. Finally, some concluding comments from the interviewees:

> 'Interpreters should be available to assist if candidates did not understand the question. It would give better access. Also even if candidates can read and understand the question as they were taught in school...they can still feel uneasy to write [the answer] because of difficulties with English. A Deaf student could give the answer to the interpreter, then the interpreter could translate it into a written paper. It would depend on the Deaf student's attitude but I think it would be the Deaf student's right to choose, if they didn't want to write. English is a second language for Deaf students while

> for hearing students it is a first language and written English is easier for them…'

> 'Deaf people should have the right to an extra hour for writing [answers] in English and to be able to get teachers or an interpreter to explain the questions in ISL. Teachers should have ISL skills before teaching in St. Joseph's…'

> 'A group should get together to help each other to learn, to prepare for exams. It would be worth it to develop good English skills for the future…'

[*Note*: This interviewee had done 'self-directed study' because she was a day-pupil and although she never worked with Deaf students to prepare as a group, she believed that the group work done by residential students helped them a lot.]

> 'Deaf students need to be well prepared for exams by studying how to break down questions and by practising questions from previous examinations…'

In summary, after their own experiences, interviewees wanted the next Deaf generation to have better access and advice and to have better preparation for their examinations. The interviewees had a strong belief in the importance of English and, further, that the use of writing in examinations proved to society that they could be equal with hearing people. Some participants support the use of ISL in examinations. However, they were not familiar with the theory and practice of using ISL in examination settings, perhaps because of their exposure to and experience of a strong oral tradition in the schools.

Discussion and implications

The initial prediction was that there would be major differences between older and younger deaf people in their attitude towards, and experiences of, examinations. This was not the case. Both groups responded in very similar ways. This may have been because the system of education provision has not changed; there remains a strong tradition of teaching through oral methods. The participants went through the pressure of oral education and this may have led to difficulties in acquiring English. In my own view and as a result of my own experiences in education, I believe that oral education also leads to poor grammar in written English. There also seems to be over reliance on the teachers in examination preparations.

It is interesting to note that the participants believed in the importance of English rather than ISL. They wanted to 'prove to society' that they could write and wanted to be equal to hearing people in order to live in the same society. The question here is who benefits from the emphasis on written English skills in examinations—the students or society? The fact is that their skills in using English should be for the students' own benefit. The reason for wanting to be able to have access in English is because the English language is everywhere: in TV teletext, newspapers, books and all kinds of public information. Also, the interviewees wanted to be able to communicate with hearing people via writing. This view seems rather limited as examination performance hardly produces equality and is unlikely to solve general access problems in society.

Four participants said that they wouldn't wish to use sign language in public examinations. One reason is that no opportunity to use ISL for examination purposes was provided in school; there was no choice for students and they had no opportunity of testing whether sign language provided better access to examinations. They had become used to writing and may have had no confidence in the idea of using video because they simply had no experience of doing so.

This has implications for all Deaf schools where the oral system is still very strong. Parents of deaf children may be misinformed by hearing professionals or given a medical perspective influencing their view, i.e. hoping to create a 'normal' situation for their child with the expectation of mixing with hearing peers. Parents like to hear about such a future for their children. The parents hope their child will achieve speech.

In this study, Deaf students had become used to sitting for written examinations and had no confidence in doing them through ISL on video. If ISL had been recognised a long time ago, interviewees could have had access to both options. If ISL was introduced in the curriculum, Deaf students would gain benefits, which would help them to achieve their potential in second level examinations and the pressure would have been less.

Nearly 40 years of public examinations have existed in Deaf schools but there has been little progress because there is a lack of options for Deaf students in accessing the examinations. Hearing people have two languages—English and Irish—and have the option as to which language to use for answering in their examinations. If hearing people can choose between Irish or English, it is surprising that Deaf people cannot choose between ISL and English. The Deaf school also provides speech and auditory training in the curriculum but does not offer Deaf Studies or courses in Deaf history or culture. However, in recent years some small steps have been taken in this direction. A module in Sign Language Studies is now included in the Leaving Certificate Applied course. But Irish Sign Language and Deaf Studies remain excluded from other public examination courses. It seems that the examination system continues to be driven by hearing options. The situation of Deaf people is hardly taken into account.

It is interesting to consider why waivers are offered to Deaf students in certain subjects and in certain parts of the examinations. For example, Deaf students are exempted from Irish and from the oral component of examinations in language subjects. Does this indicate a lower expectation of achievement for Deaf students by comparison with hearing students. Is it to make up for the lack of subject choice? Does it indicate a cover-up by the schools to avoid criticism of the poor quality of education? The waiver is not helpful, rather than being an option for Deaf people, it hides a weakness in the educational opportunities offered to Deaf people. What deaf young people need is not the chance to opt out, but rather the possibility to progress their knowledge through their own language and to be assessed in their own language.

The history of education and assessment in Ireland is long and complex. We can see the evolution of a complicated system to examine and accredit young people. Deaf children are now meant to follow a similar curriculum and usually to take the same examinations. However, as we have seen, the impact on young Deaf people is quite different, their preparation, expectation and performance are all different. It seems that a new approach to examinations may be needed.

Conclusions

We can see that the Deaf students in this small group were frustrated by the difficulties they experienced in the examination process. On the basis of what the students have said we could suggest (i) that they are experiencing considerable stress, (ii) that they are disadvantaged compared with students whose primary language is English, and (iii) that lack of access to the examination task probably leads to poorer examination results than might be expected. The results of this research suggest that we need to re-think our approach to examination preparations and procedures, especially if more bilingual education is available and if we are really serious about enabling deaf children and young people to achieve their potential. It is an issue that demands urgent investigation.

Notes

1. The Department of Education was set up in 1924, two years after the establishment of the Irish Free State. The Intermediate and Leaving Certificate examinations were introduced in 1924 (Coolahan 1981).
2. Day Vocational or Group Certificate examinations were first held in 1947. These were designed for candidates who took two year 'continuation education' courses in vocational schools. Literacy, numeracy and a range of technical subjects were examined (*ibid*).

References

Coolahan, J. (1981) *Irish Education: History and Structure*, Dublin: Institute of Public Administration.

Department of Education (1972) *The Education of Children Who are Handicapped by Impaired Hearing*, Dublin: The Stationery Office.

Village life: Deaf culture in contemporary Ireland

Patrick Matthews and Susan M. Foley-Cave

Introduction

The collective lives of Irish Deaf people as a cultural phenomenon have rarely been touched upon in any great depth with the exception of the 1996 Survey Report on education, language and culture titled *The Irish Deaf community* (Matthews 1996) and on Deaf humour (Foley-Cave 2003). Research within and on the Irish Deaf community has really only begun to take place since the early 1990s. This research, both published and unpublished, has tended to focus primarily on issues such as pedagogic practices for deaf children (St. Joseph's School for Deaf Boys 1957; Department of Education 1972, 1995; Irish Deaf Society 1986; McDonnell 1992; McDonnell and Saunders 1993; O'Reilly 1993; Griffney 1994; Swan 1994; Broderick and Duggan 1996; Crean 1997), the linguistics of Irish Sign Language (LeMaster 1990; McDonnell 1996; Matthews 1996a; Leeson 1996; 2001; O'Baoill and Matthews 2001), sociolinguistics (Burns 1995), culture (Matthews 1996b); social issues and policy-making (Scott-Gibson 1986; Griffney 1987; Irish Deaf Society 1993; Burns, Matthews and Nolan-Conroy 2001; Conama and Grehan 2002) and personal accounts of the Deaf experience (Cradden 1994; Matthews 1995).

This paper sets out to give both an emical (Deaf perspective) and etical (hearing perspective) descriptive account of ethnographic fieldwork within the Irish Deaf community. Drawing on empirical data, the paper sets out to explore issues surrounding identity politics, cultural values, community practices and intercultural fissions and fusions between Deaf 'locals' and hearing (non-deaf) people on the fringe of contemporary Deaf cultural life in Ireland.

Conceptualising the Deaf community

When one thinks of 'community' a group of people sharing the same geographical location comes to mind. The Irish Deaf community is scattered throughout Irish 'hearing' society. According to the most recent census, there are approximately 5100 Deaf people on the island of Ireland who use sign language as their preferred mode of communication (Matthews 1996:11). However, not all deaf people consider themselves to be part of, or are considered to be members of the Deaf community. Those who have become deaf through presbycusis (i.e. old age) for example, have already formed a cultural identity with mainstream Irish society, that is, they do not share the same experience or language as Deaf signers (Higgins 1980).

Deaf people who socialise with other culturally Deaf signers share a sense of *communitas*, based on a collective shared experience. The term 'community' is often used by groups of people to express their shared sense of belonging without them necessarily having to share the same geographical space. Anderson (1983) uses the phrase, 'imagined communities' to refer to how populations dispersed over a wide area can conceptualise or imagine themselves to be part of the same national community. Researchers in the field of Deaf Studies (Ladd 2003; Foley-Cave 2003) have drawn on Anderson's hypothesis. Foley-Cave (2003:9) notes:

> The Irish Deaf community can be described in terms of an 'imagined village.' That is, while the Deaf Community is demographically disjunctured, there is a 'small town mentality' where most Deaf people know each other and take an interest in the goings on within their community.

While it is common practice to use the signifier 'hearing community,' there are of course many diverse groups of people throughout the world within that one appellation. Even when referring to hearing people in Ireland, we may fall into the trap of labelling all hearing people as if they form a single homogenous entity. For ease of reference however, here we will continue to use the identity marker 'hearing community' to refer to the non-Deaf Irish majority as signified by Deaf people, that is, 'not one of us.'

As with the term 'hearing community,' the Irish Deaf community is often referred to in the singular as if it was one homogenous group. As well as the Dublin Deaf community with over 1000 Deaf members (Matthews 1996:11), there are other, smaller Deaf communities established in the major Irish towns and cities, such as those Deaf communities of Cork, Kerry and Galway to name but a few. Traditionally, these communities have established Deaf clubs and associations in order to facilitate their members' social and communicative needs.

Attributes of a community member

While allowing for individuality within the Deaf community, Deaf people collectively see the world differently to hearing people, and have specific characteristics unique to their group and express their sense of culture in a number of ways. The culturally Deaf person's experience of being 'Deaf' is not that of one who cannot hear, but that of one who is 'Deaf Proud.' This signifies a celebration of deafness, not as a person lacking ability, but as a positive state of being and a marker of in-group identity. Smith (2002) says that common historical experiences and memories play a vital part in shaping identity and culture. Collectively, Irish Deaf people express this unique identity and culture through the shared modality of Irish Sign Language.

At face value, the Deaf-Hearing identity is in binary opposition: DEAF equals 'one of us' and HEARING equals 'one of them.' However, a more complex set of relations between the Deaf and hearing signers is evident. In 'slips of the hand' some Deaf people have made distinctions between hearing signers and the ability to hear, sometimes forgetting that the person is hearing. An interesting phenomenon occurs where it is a source of honour and pride for a hearing signer to be mistaken by a Deaf person as being Deaf. However, should a hearing person mistake a Deaf person as hearing, it would be considered an insult.

A distinction arises between who qualifies as a member of the Deaf community and who is not only a member but also possesses 'Deaf culture.' Further on we will examine what is meant when we refer to Deaf culture. As with any community, there are members who may not necessarily possess all cultural traits but who do come together due to shared interests. Therefore, it is not only Deaf people who form membership of the Deaf community. Under certain conditions, there is the possibility of hearing people becoming partial members of the Deaf community.

Full membership of the Irish Deaf community requires that its members have at least some level of diminished hearing, yet the amount of hearing loss is unimportant. The most important criterion is what Baker and Padden (1978:4) have called 'attitudinal deafness':

> The most basic criteria for membership of the Deaf community is what is called 'attitudinal deafness.' This is where a person identifies as being part of the community and the other members of that community accepts that person as being a fellow member.

Ladd (2003:42) outlines three main routes for Deaf people to gain membership of the American and British Deaf Communities. Ladd's framework appears to fit the Irish context. The first route refers to the 10% of Deaf people whose one or both parents are also Deaf. This Deaf lineage may consist of deaf children, aunts, cousins, grandparents, etc. There are no exact figures for the percentage of hereditary deafness amongst the Irish Deaf population. However, informal knowledge suggests the figure to be far less that the commonly referred to 10%, which would put the number of Irish Deaf people with a Deaf lineage at about 500. A more realistic percentage would be more in the region of 5% or less.

The second route to membership occurs through the peer acculturation process of deaf pupils who attended Deaf schools and units. Ironically it is within these educational establishments, which historically played such a prominent role in the attempted assimilation of deaf children into hearing society, that many deaf children of hearing families—up to 90% of the Deaf population—are socialised into the norms of the Irish Deaf community.

The third route consists of those Deaf people who as children attended mainstream schools and later learned to sign and find their way into the Deaf community. The trend of mainstreaming deaf children into local community schools has dramatically increased in recent times. While this allows for the physical integration of the deaf child within his/her family and immediate community, in reality this

is not always the result achieved. According to ethnographic accounts
here in Ireland, access to appropriate Deaf role models, identification with other deaf children and early cultural acquisition leading to healthy self-identity is undermined (Swan 1994; Matthews 1996).

According to Matthews (1996:24), the Irish Deaf community may include people who are not themselves deaf but who actively support and co-operate with the Deaf community in the realization of their goals. Deaf people who do not see themselves as culturally Deaf or do not have a strong Deaf identity but who are involved at a basic level are also part of the Deaf community. Membership has relatively fluid rules and a few centrally held identity markers, namely, diminished hearing and ISL as the preferred language for discourse. This is illustrated by the extent to which hearing people may be accepted as partial members of the Deaf community. Partial membership may also be extended to hearing people who have a Deaf lineage and to other people that are a constant in Deaf people's lives. This is discussed further below.

Acceptance or non-acceptance of hearing people as partial members of the Deaf community is largely dependant on the kind of past experiences Deaf people have had with the hearing majority as well as the hearing person's ability to sign and frequency of attendance at Deaf events. A hearing signer with a 'good' attitude is considered by some Deaf people to be a member of the Deaf community. The importance of 'attitude' warrants further discussion.

'Good' attitude, 'bad' attitude

The concept of whether one has a 'good' or 'bad' attitude is often discussed amongst Deaf people. In Deaf culture, a hearing person with a good attitude acknowledges and respects Deaf people's ability to make autonomous decisions based on the emic knowledge of what is best for the community. He/she also respects ISL but does not necessarily have to be proficient in signing. A hearing person with a 'bad' attitude, irrespective of his/her signing abilities, negates all the qualities associated with a good attitude. The former would be perceived by Deaf people as holding paternalistic views and of seeing Deaf people in terms of being unable to make informed decisions of their own.

However, when a Deaf person is said to have a 'good' attitude, it is an affirmation of the Deaf person's commitment to and solidarity with the group. This person is proud of ISL and is perceived to be proficient in its use. A Deaf person with a good attitude assists other Deaf people to achieve the aims of the whole community. On the other hand, the Deaf person with a 'bad' attitude is one who is perceived not to participate in Deaf organised events. In fact, such a person may be disparagingly referred to as 'hearing.' That is, he/she does not share the collective values of the Deaf community.

Hearing children of Deaf parents are not audiologically deaf, but they are closer to acquiring Deaf culture fortuitously than other hearing people in the Deaf community. Although hearing children of Deaf parents do not attend the Deaf schools nor acquire world knowledge primarily through the sense of sight, nor face the same political or social marginalisation experienced by Deaf people collectively, they are nonetheless touched by the Deaf experience in a very unique way. As adults, some of these hearing people work within the Deaf community. For example, they may go on to become professional sign language interpreters, building on the cross-communication skills they may have used whilst growing up hearing in a Deaf family.

The majority of hearing people in Ireland do not know ISL, but since ISL is the most accessible way for Deaf people to express themselves, a language and cultural mediator is required in the guise of the ISL/English interpreter. The ISL/English interpreter not only facilitates the communication between two diverse language users, he/she mediates between a minority and majority social groups.

Recent times have seen an increased interest in learning ISL amongst hearing people, the reasons for which vary. Some hearing parents and siblings are now striving to acquire a language that will enable them to communicate with their deaf children. Deaf adults have assisted this process, which in turn has fostered greater understanding between hearing and Deaf people for the betterment of deaf children. Hearing colleagues of Deaf people, professionals in the health or social services, may also wish to develop signing skills. Some people who initially may have had no explicit reason for attending sign language classes may stay in contact with Deaf people and become active and beneficial contributors within and to the Deaf community.

Community activism

There are a number of organisations within the Deaf community whose actions and policies have implications for the lives of Deaf people. Metaphorically, they make up the local community council. The two main agencies in Ireland are the Irish Deaf Society (IDS) and the National Association for Deaf People (NAD). The ethos of these two organisations is seen to differ. While the NAD is regarded more as a provider of services to the Irish Deaf community, the IDS has taken on a human rights agenda, highlighting its members societal needs, promoting equality and the empowerment of all sectors of the Deaf community through 'upholding the status of Irish Sign Language and its related culture and norms.'

Deaf people express group solidarity by active participation in Deaf groups and organisations. Deaf people come together both informally and through more formal social groups such as national network of Deaf clubs, among them the Kerry Deaf Resource Centre, the Mid-West Deaf Association, Cork Association for the Deaf, Deaf Women's Groups, Deaf Men's Groups; the Irish Deaf Sports Association, the Dublin Theatre of the Deaf; the Deaf Folk Dance Group, the Deaf Art and Culture Society, the Dublin Deaf Association, the Rainbow (Deaf/ Blind) Club and Greenbow (Deaf Gay/Lesbian Association) to name but a few. Through these formally structured social outlets, Deaf people can escape from the sometimes comical, but more often than not frustrating, communicative manoeuvrings with the 'hearing world.'

Traditionally the Deaf club has been the information focal point for community activities. People came to Deaf clubs to chat with other Deaf people and to find out about up and coming events. While Deaf clubs still hold an important place within Deaf community life, there has been a decline in the numbers of younger Deaf people attending Deaf club events. Due to technological advancements, there is no longer the same need to attend the Deaf club. Instead, Deaf people use other ways of sourcing information, such as Deaf magazines, Deaf Ireland e-mail group, Hints and Deaf Info on teletext, 'Hands On' (the Deaf news programme), and text messaging. The public house has now become the unofficial 'Deaf club' where many of the younger Deaf generation go to meet up with their Deaf friends. Having said that, organised Deaf events in clubs are still well attended. Deaf people are willing to travel great distances to participate in these Deaf events within Ireland or abroad in order to meet other Deaf people. The bonds of friendship that Deaf people make during their school years create not only lifelong relationships with each other, but also enable the continuation and maintenance of their social community.

Historically, the Roman Catholic Church and the Church of Ireland have played a significant role in the lives of many Irish Deaf people. Since the mid-1800s, the Christian Brothers have managed St. Joseph's School for Deaf Boys and the Dominican Order has administered St. Mary's School for Deaf Girls. On leaving school Deaf people were often assisted in seeking employment by their religious educators. However, within the last three decades the direct influence of the Catholic Church on the lives of Deaf people has declined. The Catholic Institute of the Deaf owns the premises of the Dublin Deaf Club in Drumcondra, Dublin. Traditionally, it was expected that representatives from religious orders be invited to the marriages of Deaf couples and be present at christenings and funerals. Today, this trend is shifting as attitudes and values change (Healy 2003). According to the 2002 census (Irish Independent, 2003), 11.6% of the Irish population practices other religions or have no particular faith. The influx of immigrants and refugees in recent years has contributed to this percentage. This may be reflected amongst Deaf people where they are beginning to encounter other spiritual experiences, paralleling the change of attitudes in contemporary Irish society.

Valuing Deaf culture

The notion of culture, has taken on political significance in more recent years, dominating discourses on feminism, revolutionary nationalism and ethnicity. Eagleton (2000:10) says that 'culture in the broad sense of identity, value, sign, language, life-style, shared history, belonging or solidarity, is the very language in which one articulates one's political demands.' Deaf discourse centres around key signs such as DEAF CULTURE, DEAF THEIR SIGN, ISL, DEAF COMUNITY and DEAF WAY. Deaf community members see Deaf people who 'have' Deaf culture as being an intrinsic part of their Deaf community (Foley-Cave 2003:13). Deaf people who have Deaf culture are automatic members of the Deaf community but not all members of the Deaf community can or even need to have Deaf culture although they must know and respect it and those who have it.

There is a high rate of endogamous marriages within the Deaf community and young Deaf men and women tend to live with or close by one another, particularly in the larger towns and cities. Ladd (2003:42) suggests an intermarriage rate of 90% amongst Deaf people in Britain. As there are similar experiences amongst Irish Deaf people in terms of mode of communication and educational experiences, this figure serves as a rough estimation of marriage patterns amongst the Irish Deaf population. In recent times with more hearing people learning to sign, anecdotal evidence suggests that the number of Deaf/hearing relationships has increased. It is important to note that the hearing partner's fluency in ISL and awareness of Deaf culture not only allows for the possibility of developing a relationship with a Deaf person, but also greatly enhances the possibility of sustaining the cross-cultural relationship.

The majority of Deaf people spend their working week in the company of hearing people who, for the most part, do not possess fluency in ISL. Therefore, Deaf community activities such as some of those mentioned above, are seen as vital outlets for the mental and emotional well being of the group. At these events, Deaf people catch up on the latest news and swap stories and anecdotes of miscommunications. Deaf people discuss the silly things that hearing people do which may be referred to as HEARING THEIR-WAY. This could be translated as, 'Sure, what more could you expect. They're hearing after all.' This sentiment said in jest is best illustrated by the following anecdote (Foley-Cave 2003:21):

> A couple of years back, a Deaf woman needed to make a telephone call. This was before there was text messaging. She went to the General Post Office on O'Connell Street and handed a note to a Hearing woman, saying she was Deaf and could this woman make the call for her and relay her message. Obligingly, the Hearing woman placed the coins in the telephone slot, dialled the number, handed the telephone to the Deaf woman and left!

 There is a strong sense of collective responsibility amongst Irish Deaf people. Deaf people actively encourage hearing parents of deaf children to sign as well as acting as linguistic and cultural role models for their deaf children. Much political activism by the Irish Deaf community focuses on access and education. Politically motivated Deaf people have done postgraduate research on topics as varied as social policy and the Deaf citizen, human rights, access to information through ISL, improvement in the subtitling service and better employment opportunities. Deaf and hearing community members lobby to improve the quality of education and literacy skills of deaf children. It is quite common for young Deaf men and women to take on leadership roles in Deaf summer camps, scouts and drama to actively encourage deaf children to achieve their full potential by providing them with positive Deaf role models.

Deaf people are often perceived by hearing people to be highly competitive, even aggressively so, particularly in sport. Intra group competitiveness is not obviously marked amongst Irish Deaf people, except when an Irish Deaf team plays against a Deaf team from abroad. The 'aggressiveness' that hearing people perceive is when Deaf people are competing against a hearing side. A young Deaf footballer told how St. Vincent's (an Irish Deaf soccer team) had just beaten a 'hearing' team. When asked naively the name of the hearing team, the incredulous response was, 'I don't know. They were hearing!' Such sentiments are an example of the pride and importance of Deaf people winning out over the hearing majority. It also highlights the relative insignificance of English names and titles amongst Deaf people.

Deaf and hearing people who have prolonged contact with the Deaf community are given name signs by the Deaf members. These are sign symbols unique to that Deaf or hearing person. The hearing person new to the Deaf community does not automatically receive a name sign. This process takes time with the name fingerspelt or the first letter of the person's name used until Deaf people get to know the hearing person better and a name is then chosen. It is rare that a hearing person would give him/herself a name sign. Even if this were the case, the hearing person's self-chosen name sign would fall into disuse and a new name given instead. Below are some of the ways in which name signs are created. They may be based on:

- the person's physical character, e.g. wears glasses, has curly hair or red cheeks;
- a particular habit, e.g. bites her thumbnail;
- the person's emotional characteristic or state of being, e.g. is always late, fussy, smiling;
- the first letter of the person's first name and surname, e.g. M-C;
- the first letter of the person's first name only, e.g. S;
- a reduced fingerspelling of the person's first name, e.g. #PAT;
- the spelling of the person's first or surname, e.g. Angela may be given the sign for 'angel';
- a descriptive marker, e.g. the Deaf person's mother, son, husband.

Hearing people often comment that Deaf people do not have a sense of humour. This is a fallacy. It is true that humour especially based on English word play is not amusing to Deaf people, largely due to its use of assonance and alliteration and the idea of sharing a sense of being in the world through sound. Deaf people's sense of humour, like their language, is primarily visual. Slapstick humour is considered quite hilarious, as is mimicry of the Deaf or hearing person's characteristics. The targets of many ethnic jokes are found in the majority culture—Apache Indians base part of their humour on Anglo-Americans (Basso 1979). In Deaf culture the joker's target is often found in the hearing community or in miscommunications that ensue between Deaf and hearing people. The following joke (Foley-Cave 2003:8) is an example of this:

> A Cuban, a Russian and a Deaf man are on a train. The Cuban lights up his cigars and after a short while, chucks them out the window. The other two ask him why he did that. He replies, 'I am Cuban. We have plenty of cigars in Cuba.' The Russian meanwhile starts knocking back the vodkas. Again after a time, he throws all his vodka out the train window. When asked why, he says, 'I am Russian. In Russia we have plenty of vodka.' finally, the Deaf man picks up his interpreter and throws her out the window. Aghast, the other two ask what he did that for. He replies, 'The interpreter is Hearing. We have plenty of Hearing people in the world!'

 Within the Deaf community, stories have been passed from older Deaf people to the younger Deaf generation. Some of these stories may have their origins based in fact but over the years the tale has slowly changed so that the truth or falsehood of the original story is no longer known. These stories maybe based on school experiences involving the Christian Brothers or Dominican Sisters at Dublin's two main boarding schools for deaf children. Other stories revolve around Deaf people's experiences at work or perhaps unusual happenings. A ghost story would be a typical example of a tale that changes over time as it is told and retold time and time again. The Deaf community passes down its stories through Irish Sign Language but until quite recently (i.e. with the use of the camcorder) had no way of recording them. This has meant that some part of Deaf folklore has been lost during the period in Ireland (circa 1950s onwards) when oralism was introduced into the schools damaging much of the (pardon the expression) 'oral' tradition.

The concept of Deaf poetry is not a predominant one in Irish Deaf culture. Until the 1980s and 1990s, poetry was considered to be associated with spoken language. As travelling abroad became more frequent for the Irish Deaf population, exposure to Deaf poetry from the United States and Europe began to spark an interest in and a new understanding of poetic expression. Signed poetry manipulates the features of a language using poetic licence such as incorporating subtle handshape changes and smooth flowing movements in repetitive motion throughout a signed performance. As interest developed, Deaf poetry from other countries was borrowed and adapted to ISL, an example being 'The Teddy Bear' from ASL. The development of unique Irish Sign Language poetry is only just beginning. As imaginations and creativity takes flight, it is certain that the poetic talents will emerge from members of the Irish Deaf community.

Technological advances and the Deaf community

Throughout the decades we have seen many advances in the technology utilised by Deaf people. The telephone, for example was invented in the 19th century by a staunch oralist, Alexander Graham Bell, while he was attempting to develop a hearing aid device for his deaf mother and wife. It was not until recent years that Deaf people finally gained their first access to telephone technology via the 'minicom' (text phone)—a device that records incoming and outgoing messages by placing the receiver on a machine that encodes and decodes typed messages. Access was limited to people who also had a 'minicom.' Most hearing people did not own one so a 'relay service' was established to accommodate message transfers between Deaf and hearing people with an intermediary relaying the typed message to the Deaf customer and the spoken message to the hearing customer. Many, however, felt that this arrangement was unsatisfactory.

The fax machine was improvement on this mode of communication. However, the more recent introduction of mobile text messaging provides Deaf people with more complete access to communication channels between Deaf and hearing people. The internet and e-mail also provide Deaf people with user-friendly ways of communicating and accessing information. The one drawback with all of the above devices is that information must be communicated in English—a second language for most Irish Deaf people. The future however promises new ways of communicating through sign language. Already mobile phones are being introduced that include picture messaging. The next logical technological step is to allow motion picture imaging for mobile phones. The videophone uses this concept at present and, while current devices do not reproduce images clear enough for signed discourse, the future seems promising.

Other types of Deaf technology include doorbells that produce a visual signal by flashing the house lights. This system can also be connected to the telephone and fax. Other devices include vibrating or flashing alarm clocks as well as vibrating devices that can be worn on the belt and can alert the Deaf person to a baby's cry, a fire alarm or a doorbell. Red flashing lights are now added to the typical smoke alarm units found in places of employment. Television channels subtitle some of their programmes although this service is by no means fully developed.

Social codes of contact

Every culture forms collectively agreed patterns of behaviour. Failure to adhere to these social laws could end in chastisement and rejection of the offender by the social group. One such example amongst Irish people is their dislike of finger pointing. A natural gesture used by children when gaining an adult's attention, is soon curtailed after regular displays of disapproval by the adults. However, pointing, known linguistically as 'indexing,' is an important feature of ISL and an accepted part of Deaf culture.

Each society develops different forms of phatic communication—greetings, making small talk, and so on. Many Deaf cultural norms centre on social phenomena such as introductions, salutations, initiating a conversation, and gaining another's attention. It is at these times that the accepted behaviours of Deaf people differ significantly from those of the rest of Irish society. Some of these social norms are culturally and group determined whilst others, such as the importance of eye contact in a signed conversation, are linguistically determined. Deaf children usually acquire this communicative competence through early contact with other Deaf people, such as parents, siblings, peers and other role models. Should children miss out on this socialisation process, as adults they will quickly adjust in order to be accommodated by established members of the Deaf community.

Where the social behaviours of Irish Deaf and hearing people differ, these differences are so culturally embedded that people are unaware of them in any conscious way. They are simply 'what we do.' If one is unaware of these differing behaviours, misunderstandings and conflicts between Deaf and hearing people may ensue. There are, for example, certain steps to follow when creating, maintaining and terminating a signed conversation. The general rules to follow when one initiates a conversation involve important features of communicative competence in Irish Deaf culture. The particular course of action depends on the setting and how many people's attention one wants to attract. To get one person's attention you may:

- wave your hand low in signing space;
- bang the table / staircase, etc, only if the person's body is in contact with it;
- wave your hand to gain attention when you enter a room, office, etc.
- tap the person's shoulder gently; never tap the person's back or head or approach too abruptly as this can cause alarm;
- if the person is sitting too far away to tap the shoulder, then it is

appropriate to tap his/her knee;
- if you know the person well, then it is also acceptable to touch the hand or lower part of arm below the elbow to gain attention.

To gain the attention of a group you may...

- wave both hands vigorously;
- switch lights on and off once; this can also be used as a way of 'knocking' when entering a room;
- stamp a wooden floor with your foot;
- use other members to gain the whole group's attention by creating a 'domino' effect, i.e. get one to tap another to get attention.

Once you have gained your audience's attention, wait until you have eye contact before starting your signed conversation. Maintaining eye contact is essential in signed discourse and is further discussed below. It is important to maintain an equal eye-level. If the conversation is lengthy where one is sitting you may wish to ask your signing partner to take a seat opposite you or you may choose to stand. Allow a comfortable distance between you and your interlocutor to assist smooth dialogue.

Eye contact is extremely important. Once you have gained your signing partner's eye-gaze, the next step is to maintain it. When signing it is normal to divert one's eye-gaze in accordance with the rules of ISL grammar. However, the signer's audience must continue to watch what is being articulated. If eye contact is broken, the signer may turn in the direction of their signing partner's gaze to see why his/her attention has been directed away from the conversation. If this happens more than once in the signed discourse, it indicates boredom or lack of interest. Whether or not the signer's audience is bored to tears with the conversation is of little concern; breaking eye contact is considered very rude. Life, being what it is, there has to be an exception to every rule so if there is something unusual going on out of the signer's sight, then you would be forgiven for diverting your eye-gaze. However, you would inform the person as to the reason why you broke eye contact.

Visibility is of prime importance as it is through vision that the majority of Deaf people acquire information. Therefore, at any event where there are Deaf people, a meeting or conference, for example, there is much movement of chairs, tables and other visual obstructions until such time as all Deaf people present can see the presenter or interpreter. It is quite appropriate and necessary for Deaf people to rearrange the environment to facilitate access to the signed discourse. Deaf people who regularly attend meetings and who wish to make a contribution will usually move to the front of the room in order to be clearly visible to the rest of the attendees. Should inexperienced or shy people prefer to stay where they are, then their questions or comments will be either relayed to the others present, or they will be told in no uncertain terms to move to the front of the group.

Hearing people new to the ways of the Deaf community may find it strange to be asked ARE-YOU DEAF? This conversation opener acts as both an identity marker and as a communication guide. The function of asking 'Are you Deaf?' is twofold. Firstly, the Deaf person is really asking, 'Are you one of us?' It is a way of finding out what kind of social relationship one is to expect or whether or not the meeting is likely to be based on a shared educational background, mutual solidarity and common difficulties in communicating with the wider society.

Secondly, 'Are you Deaf?' determines how the conversation should proceed. If the person says he/she is Deaf then the conversation will continue in a naturally free flowing signed discourse. If the person says he/she is hearing, then the Deaf signer's style will change to a more English structured modality, possibly with increased mouthing of English words and the greater use of fingerspelling. This accommodation technique is employed to make the hearing signer feel more comfortable. Most Deaf people are well used to accommodating hearing people in their daily interactions so that code switching becomes second nature. It has been noted by fluent signers that where the normal Deaf conversation opener 'Are you Deaf?' is omitted for some reason, on the Deaf person's discovery that the person is hearing, the conversation will change from the natural signing flow of ISL to a more English-like structure.

Noises such as running fingernails across a blackboard or a persistent car alarm distract and irritate hearing people. For Deaf people visual 'noise' distracts. Examples of this include swinging legs while sitting, a flickering light, or having to watch someone with brightly patterned clothes signing for a long period of time. The following is a list of other behaviours that are considered impolite in Deaf culture:

- 'Listening in' on a signed conversation without joining in; whether the person is a signer or not is irrelevant;
- Staring—this poses some difficulty for hearing people new to the Deaf community since one of the best ways of acquiring ISL is to watch native signers in conversation; to avoid any misunderstandings it is wise to ask if it is okay to watch the conversation;
- Poking someone with an object such as a pen to gain their attention;
- Signing or talking while someone else is signing—appropriate turn taking is highly regarded in most cultures; to signal you wish to interpose, wiggle your hand or raise your index finger, then wait your turn;
- Placing your hands on someone to stop that person signing is a definite cultural blunder comparable with placing your hands over someone's mouth whilst that person is speaking;
- Holding an object such as a cigarette, knife, fork or pen in your hand while signing is also distracting as it interferes with clear communication;
- Averting eye-gaze from the signer whilst participating in a signed conversation; it denotes lack of interest in what the person has to say;
- Last but not least, hearing signers who speak while there are Deaf people present thereby exclude the latter from the conversation.

Conclusion

This paper aimed to gave an overall descriptive account of the Irish Deaf community in present day Ireland. While there have been many changes both within and outside the Deaf community, what remains constant is that there continues to be a dynamic Deaf culture. From the perspective of the Deaf community, there is an emerging openness to allow hearing people enter into the Deaf world although this may often be a partial rather than an absolute acceptance. From the perspective of hearing society, there is a slowly growing recognition and respect for the views and opinions of Irish Deaf people as colleagues, friends and advocates.

References

Anderson, B. (1983) *Imagined Communities: Reflections on the Origins and Spread of Nationalism*, London: Verso and New Left Books.

Baker, C. and Padden, C. (1978) *American Sign Language: A Look at its Story, Structure and Community*, Silver Spring, MD: T.J. Publishers Inc.

Basso, K. (1979) *Portraits of 'The White Man': Linguistic Play and Cultural Symbols among the Western Apache*, Cambridge: Cambridge University Press.

Broderick, T. and Duggan, R. (1996) *St. Mary's School for Deaf Girls 1846–1996*, Dublin: St. Mary's School for Hearing Impaired Girls, Cabra, Dublin.

Burns, S. (1995) *Irish Sign Language in a minority framework, unpublished* M. Sc. dissertation, Dublin: University of Dublin, Trinity College.

Burns, S., Matthews, P. A. and Nolan-Conroy, E. (2001) Language attitudes, in C. Lucas (ed.) *The Sociolinguistics of Sign Languages*, UK: Cambridge University Press.

Conama, J. B. and Grehan, C. (2002) *Is There Poverty in the Deaf Community?* Dublin: Irish Deaf Society Publications.

Cradden, J. (1994) *I'm Deaf Too, Deaf Identity, Education and the Dublin Deaf Community*, unpublished B.A. thesis, Dublin: Dublin City University.

Crean, E. (1997) *Breaking the Silence: The Education of the Deaf in Ireland 1816–1996*, Dublin: Irish Deaf Society Publications.

Department of Education (1972) *The Education of Children Who Are Handicapped by Impaired Hearing*, Dublin: The Stationery Office.

—— (1995) *Charting our Education Future*, Dublin: The Stationery Office.

Eagleton, T. (2000) Culture Wars, in M. Maguire *et al* (eds) Dis-ease with Postmodern Anthropology, *Irish Journal of Anthropology*, 5(1), Dublin: Anthropological Association of Ireland.

Foley-Cave, S. M. (2003) *Humour-Power-Identity: An Anthropological Exploration of Irish Deaf Humour*, unpublished dissertation, Bachelor of Arts in Anthropology, Dublin: Dublin Business School.

Fromkin, V. and Rodman, R. (1998) *Introduction to Language*, New York: Harcourt Brace.

Griffey, Sr. N. (1987) *The Deaf Parishioner: A guide for priests and others in pastoral ministry*, Dublin: St. Joseph's House for Adult Deaf and Deaf/ Blind.

—— (1994) *From Silence to Speech: 50 Years with the Deaf*, Dublin: Dominican Publications.

Healy, A. (2003) Deaf society complains of 'intrusive' chaplaincy service, *Irish Times*, Thursday 16th January.

Higgins, P. (1980) *Outsiders in a Hearing World: A Sociology of Deafness*, New York: Sage.

Irish Deaf Society (1986) *Total Communication*, Dublin: Irish Deaf Society Publications.

—— (1993) *Understanding Human Rights of Irish Deaf People, Second Congress*, Dublin: Irish Deaf Society Publications.

Irish Independent, 28th June 2003.

Ladd, P. (2003) *Understanding Deaf Culture: In Search of Deafhood*, Clevedon, UK: Multilingual Matters.

Leeson, L. (1996) *The Expression of Time in Sign Language with Special Reference to Irish Sign Language*, unpublished M. Phil. in Linguistics dissertation, University of Dublin, Trinity College.

—— (2001) *Aspects of Verbal Valency in Irish Sign Language*, unpublished Ph. D. thesis, University of Dublin, Trinity College.

LeMaster, B. C. (1990) *The Maintenance and Loss of Female and Male Signs in the Dublin Deaf Community*, unpublished doctoral dissertation, University of California, Los Angeles.

Maguire, F. (1991) *A User's Guide for Irish Sign Language Research*, unpublished M. Phil. in Applied Linguistics dissertation, University of Dublin, Trinity College.

Matthews, P. A. (1995) Issues in Ireland for the Irish Deaf Community: An Insight from a Deaf Person's Perspective, in I. O'Deirg (ed.) *Teangeolas, Journal of the Linguistics Institute of Ireland*, Dublin: The Linguistics Institute of Ireland.

—— (1996a) Extending the lexicon of Irish Sign Language, in D. O'Baoill (ed.) *Teanga 16, The Irish Yearbook of Applied Linguistics*, Dublin: Irish Association of Applied Linguistics.

Matthews, P. A. (1996b) *The Irish Deaf Community, Volume 1*, Dublin: Institiuid Teangeolaiochta Eireann.

McDonnell, J. (1992) *Teaching Language to Deaf Children*, unpublished M. Phil. in Applied Linguistics dissertation, University of Dublin,

Trinity College.

—— (1996) *Verb Categories in Irish Sign Language*, unpublished Ph.D. thesis, University of Dublin, Trinity College.

McDonnell, P. and Saunders, H. (1993) Sit on your hands: Strategies to prevent signing, in R. Fischer and H. Lane (eds) *Looking Back: A Reader on the History of Deaf Communities and their Sign Languages*, Hamburg: Signum Press.

O'Baoill, D. and Matthews, P. A. (2001) *The Irish Deaf Community, Volume 2: The Structure of Irish Sign Language*, Dublin: Institiuid Teangeolaiochta Eireann.

O'Reilly, J. (1993) *The hearing impaired: Equal opportunity in higher education in Ireland? Institution and student perspectives*, unpublished M.A. thesis, National University of Ireland.

Scott-Gibson, L. (1986) Interpreting Services and Total Communication in Irish Deaf Society, *Total Communication*, Dublin: Irish Deaf Society.

Smith, Anthony D. (2002) Towards a Global Culture? in D. Held and A. McGrew (eds) *The Global Transformations Reader*, Cambridge: Polity Press.

St. Joseph's School for the Deaf. (1957) *Centenary Record 1857–1957*, St. Joseph's School for Deaf Boys, Cabra, Dublin.

Swan, E. (1994) *Study of the Dublin Schools for the Deaf*, Unpublished Report, Dublin: Catholic Institute for the Deaf.

Williams, R. (1983) *Keywords*, London: Fontana.

II SIGN LANGUAGE FUNDAMENTALS

Language processing in speech and sign: similar or different?

Dawn Duffin

Introduction: what is language processing?

Language processing, or psycholinguistics, is a relatively recent discipline and one whose corpus is expanding rapidly. This means that mainstream texts, research and reference materials must come to include the existence and relevance of signed languages within their corpuses. Crystal's 1997 definition does not consider a visio-spatial modality of language and in this is typical of many of the assumptions of mainstream research that language is speech, '...the study of the mental processes underlying the planning, production, perception and comprehension of speech' (Crystal 1997:316). Three areas within the domain of psycholinguistics that are particularly relevant to any research of signed languages are language acquisition, the relationships between cognitive and linguistic universals, and sign language processing.

Historically, the literature on cognition contains scant reference to sign languages. *The Psychology of Language* (Harley 1995), a university text on language and cognition of nearly five hundred pages, uses less than two to refer to an experiment in which chimpanzees were allegedly taught to use American Sign Language (ASL). The only other reference to signed languages is in the further reading section in Chapter 8 where the authors refer to ASL as a 'full blown language.' The 2001 edition contains this definition of American Sign Language (ASL):

> American Sign Language (ASL, sometimes called AMESLAN). ASL is the standard sign language used by people with hearing impairment in North America. Just like spoken language it has words and syntax. (Harley 2002:52)

It is relevant to mention the following points:

- ASL is no more or less standard than any spoken language; it is subject to the same vagaries of accent, dialect, socio-linguistics and language borrowing that any spoken language is.
- 'Hearing impairment' is not a term by which native users of sign language refer to themselves.
- Sign language phonology is produced in the form of signs and spoken language phonology is produced in the form of words. The common factor is that both languages use different symbols (be they signs or words) to represent the same concepts. When we use a word like *table* or a sign like TABLE we are representing the concept that we all understand.
- Any utterance of a sign language is not like any utterance of a spoken language in any way, but reflects, as does an utterance in a spoken language, a mode of articulation. Like all spoken languages, sign languages are constrained by grammar under Chomskian principles.

Similarly there is no reference to signed languages within *Human Cognitive Neuropsychology*, a reference text of several hundred pages, where less than four are devoted to the cognitive disorders of sign language users (Ellis and Young 1996), which does not give the reader any understanding that a large body of sign language users exist who communicate daily through a signed language without any cognitive difficulty.

It is now more than forty years since William Stokoe's ground-breaking 1960 description of ASL in terms of linguistic structure showed that signed languages, which had always been considered as being primarily gestural, were in fact natural languages of the same linguistic level as spoken languages. The slowly increasing number of publications that do discuss visio-spatial sign language processing in the context of its being one of at least two naturally occurring options of language modality, includes *Language Acquisition by Eye* (Chamberlain, Morford and Mayberry 2000) and *Language in Atypical Populations* (Tartter 1998). The most comprehensive discussion of signed language processing to date, from Karen Emmorey, entitled *Language, Cognition and the Brain: Insights from Sigh Language Research* appeared in June 2002.

The difficulty I have with the Crystal 1997 definition is that he uses the word 'speech' as *the* manner of language production and this disallows any alternatives. This is a trend that continues to dominate mainstream linguistic publications and is responsible for the continuing lack of awareness of the actual richness and breadth of language across modalities. Assumptions that speech is language have influenced many misplaced ideas about deafness and language and have led to inappropriate health and education services for Deaf people throughout the modern world (Duffin, forthcoming). If we change this wording to 'speech and sign' or use words like 'articulation' or 'symbol', then we stop excluding signed languages from the general linguistic discussion. For this reason I consider it more accurate to use neutral terms like 'linguistic utterances' or 'representations of language'. It can also be assumed that linguistic terms such as 'phonology' and 'morphology', previously associated with only spoken language, can now be perceived to refer to at least one other mode of language, sign language.

An utterance (something we say or sign) is a physical manifestation of a mental process. It is the underlying language processing of our utterances that allows us to produce what we wish to say so others can perceive it. These two processes are known as language production and language perception respectively. The following diagram presupposes that within the whole breadth of human cognitive processes some are related to language and, more specifically, to our innate capacity to develop language (Chomsky 1986). Chomsky hypothesises that we are hard wired for language and, have therefore, an innate capacity to acquire the language of whatever culture or country we are born into.

DIAGRAM 1: REPRESENTATIONS OF LANGUAGE (DUFFIN 1998:16)

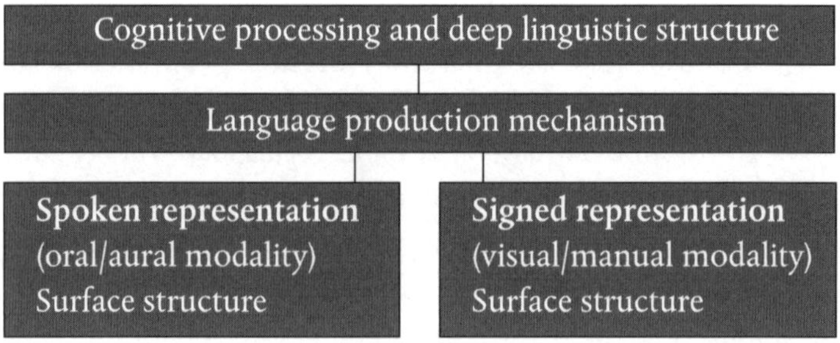

Mostly we assume that terms for language and its representations (utterances in either speech or sign) are synonymous. It is only when we start to look at the mental processes underlying our language that we start to realise that we have to decide what we want to say before we say it, and that we go through a process of selection until we find the exact arrangement of words or signs that will suit our purpose. One way of demonstrating that this is what happens is to look at the phrase 'on the tip of my tongue.' Everyone will have had the experience of searching for a particular word or phrase that he or she knows but is not accessible to him or her in its word or sign form at that time. We say, 'It's on the tip of my tongue.' I also have seen sign language users searching their minds for the sign they want. It is interesting to consider how we might describe this: 'It's in the tips of my fingers', for example?

In summary then, the process of using language in communication has a mental level where we prepare what we want to communicate and decode or comprehend what has been communicated to us, as well as an articulatory or phonological level at which we actually say a word or make a sign and see or hear that a word has been said or a sign that has been produced. Examining the relationship of these processes with each other is known as language processing or psycholinguistics. We can refer to the mental levels as the deep structures of language processing and we can refer to the phonological level as the surface structures.

We can use words like symbol, utterance, articulation or linguistic representation to refer to all the possible ways of producing the surface structures of language, which include spoken and signed forms. This is the most appropriate type of linguistic categorisation because it allows us to discuss language in general without excluding any modality of language and also because it is theoretically possible that there are other modes, manner or forms of language that have not yet been described.

Cognitive processing and deep linguistic structure

In coming to view language processing as a cognitive rather than a physical activity, we also become able to understand why one of the fundamental questions of theoretical linguistics has come to concern itself with the *how* of why we are able to understand each other through meaningful communication rather than with making accurate descriptions of discrete languages. Chomsky is the important theoretical linguist who initiated this discussion and he has continued to inform it for fifty years:

> Structuralist descriptions of the world's languages have revealed common elements and rules. Modern linguistics considers this no accident; *language universals* (the elements common to unrelated languages) are believed to arise from an innate human language 'program,' a *language acquisition device* (LAD) or *universal grammar* (UG). The hypothesis is that UG provides the infant with an unconscious idea of what language will be like, what elements and rules there can be. These innate ideas enable the appropriate abstraction of underlying language structure, with the language the child hears determining values for innately specified parameters. (Tartter 1998a:13)

Some of the cognitive processing structures concerned with language are related to the actual specific details of the particular language(s) we use. Two of these language specifics are more generally known as phonology and morphology and refer to the breakdown of a word or sign into its basic components:

> **Phonology**
> A branch of *Linguistics*, which studies the sound systems of languages. Out of the very wide range of sounds the human vocal apparatus can produce and which are studied by *Phonetics*, only a relatively small number are used distinctively in any one language. The sounds are organised into a system of contrasts, which are analysed in terms of phonemes, distinctive features or other such 'phonological units' according to the theory used (Crystal 1997,290).

Again, the above definition needs to be changed as suggested below to incorporate signed languages and therefore hold true for any given language regardless of modality:

> Out of the very wide range of sounds the human vocal apparatus *and the wide range of shapes and movements the human*

> *hands, body and face* can produce [...] The *sounds or kinetic movements* are organised into a system of contrasts...

The meaning and grammar structure of any given language is its morphology:

> **Morphology**
> The branch of grammar, which studies the structure, or forms of words, primarily through the use of the morpheme construct. It is generally divided into two fields: the study of inflections (inflectional morphology) and of word formation (derivational morphology). (Crystal 1997:249).

Once more we need to adapt the definition to serve our purpose:

> The branch of grammar which studies the structure or forms of words, or signs and non-manual features (NMF's), primarily through the use of the morpheme construct...

The terms phonology and morphology describe the smallest units of sound and meaning which form part of the processing system of a given language that allows us to understand and to create relevant and meaningful communication. This system is allowed to develop through an innate capacity during childhood in a language acquisition process that only requires an environment offering the correct input data for the hardwired language 'device.' To use a computer metaphor, it is as if the software of the language programme (LAD) is already on the hard drive but has not yet been installed. The linguistic environment into which the child is born activates the programme. It also appears that a speech option will be installed unless the circumstances exist that will trigger a sign option.

Language acquisition options

The signed language option normally applies only to deaf children born into families with Deaf parents and/or siblings. I will remind you here that as 90% of deaf children are born into hearing families, this means that most deaf children cannot follow a maximally effective first language acquisition pattern unless the hearing parents have the knowledge, skills and resources to create the appropriate environment.

 Most deaf children follow a more atypical language development pattern (centre element in Diagram 2) that we do not have leisure to discuss here but will just say a few words for the readers' interest.

Chomskian theory posits that the LAD is activated in a linguistic environment and indeed the deaf child's spoken language acquisition potential is activated but is also not able to follow the natural pattern of spoken language acquisition because there is difficulty in the sounds of spoken language being heard; the degree of access naturally varies depending on the individual's audiogram. The fact the deaf children do indeed acquire varying levels of spoken language skill is testament to the tenacity of the LAD.

The discussion here, however, is concerned with the outcomes of the models shown in the two language environments that do lead to full fluency of a primary language (the two outer elements in Diagram 2). We may ask why spoken language has apparently won out over signed language in a general sense for there is no reason why we should not all sign (see Groce 1985). I speculate when I say I think it is simply a matter of convenience. Sound is the easiest way of attracting attention. It is easier to speak whilst having one's arms occupied. It is possible to listen and watch simultaneously.[1] It does not appear that there is a preferred option for modality for language processing. If a hearing child is born to Deaf parents he or she tends to become equally bimodal and bilingual. Many interpreters are such balanced bilinguals. The language acquisition options shown in Diagram 2 demonstrate that the existence of appropriate—that is, accessible—linguistic data in the environment of the child is more critical than its modality. It seems that the LAD will use any and all of the options in the environment, so long as they can be fully accessed through a sensory channel.

We have looked at a simple model of language as a mental rule based system and discussed what conditions are necessary for the system to become fully active during child language acquisition. We have also described how the phonological and morphological relationships of children's language perception and production require the linguistic data of the environment to be fully accessible in order that a primary language can be acquired.

DIAGRAM 2: LANGUAGE ACQUISITION OPTIONS (DUFFIN 1998:8)

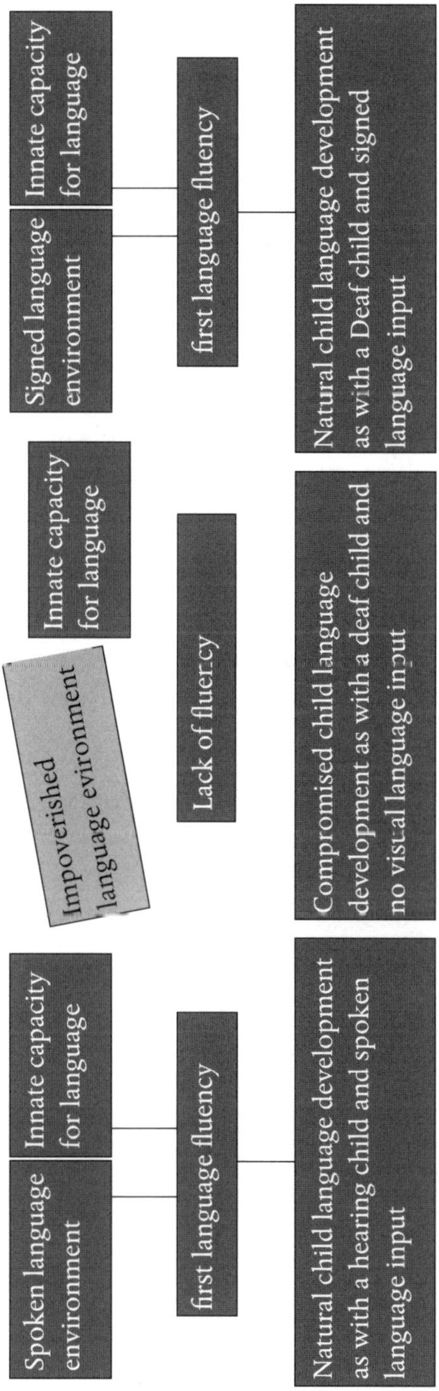

Language production and perception mechanisms

Anything we utter (word or sign) is a physical representation (or manifestation) of the end product of our decision to communicate. We decide what we wish to say, and then we say it. The actual process is incredibly fast and the decision making about what we wish to say or sign, and the actual communicating of the result of that decision making process appear to happen simultaneously in any given communication. This process is known as language production.

Our understanding of inputted language, either through ear or eye, is a similar process but in reverse. We hear or see what has been said and then we work out the meaning. This is also an incredibly fast process with no discernible time lag between a person speaking or signing to us, and our understanding of what has been communicated to us. This process is known as language perception.

We are barely aware that we follow these patterns of processing because they occur automatically and because the speed at which they take place is so rapid. I noted earlier that there were at least two modalities of language. The following diagrams show models for both aural/oral and visual/spatial modalities of linguistic processing.

DIAGRAM 3: PRODUCTION AND PERCEPTION: AURAL/ORAL MODALITY (DUFFIN 1999:94)

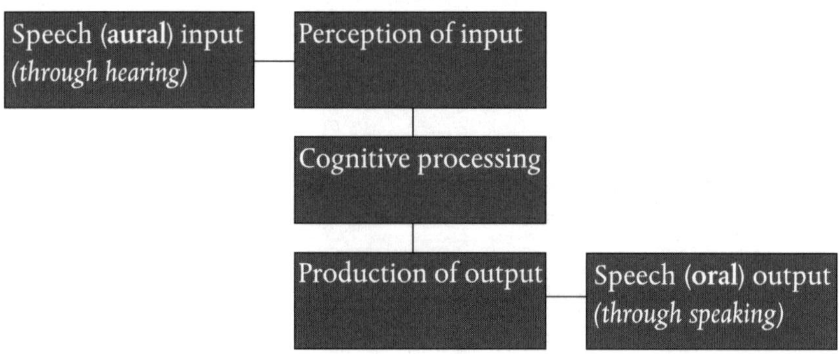

DIAGRAM 4: PRODUCTION AND PERCEPTION: VISUAL/MANUAL-SPATIAL MODALITY (DUFFIN, *ibid*).

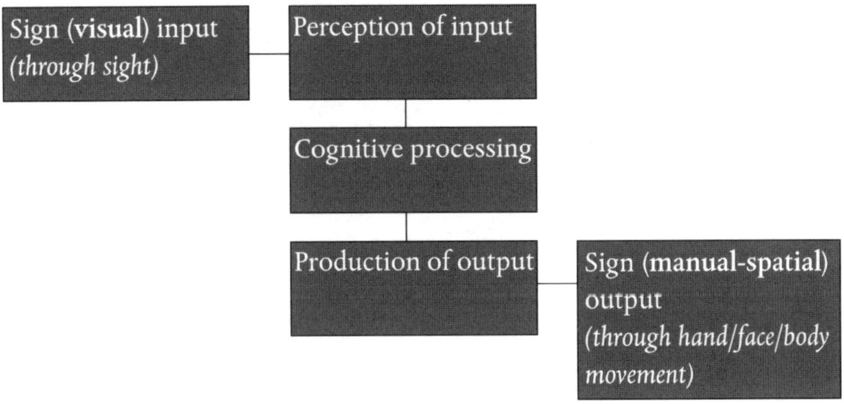

By breaking down the specialist terms of theoretical linguistics we can see that language information needs to have a pathway to the brain so it can be processed (that is, be constructed or deconstructed, or be encoded or decoded). The models for speech and sign in Diagrams 3 and 4 above can more clearly be demonstrated by making explicit reference to the physical routes as in the following two representations of the model.

DIAGRAM 5: LANGUAGE MODALITY: SPEECH

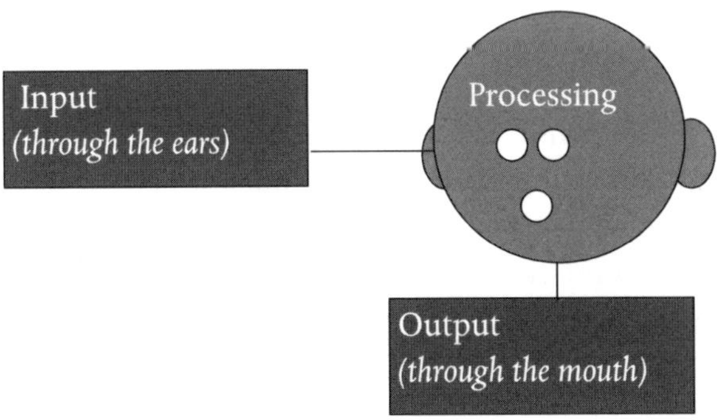

DIAGRAM 6: LANGUAGE MODALITY: SIGN

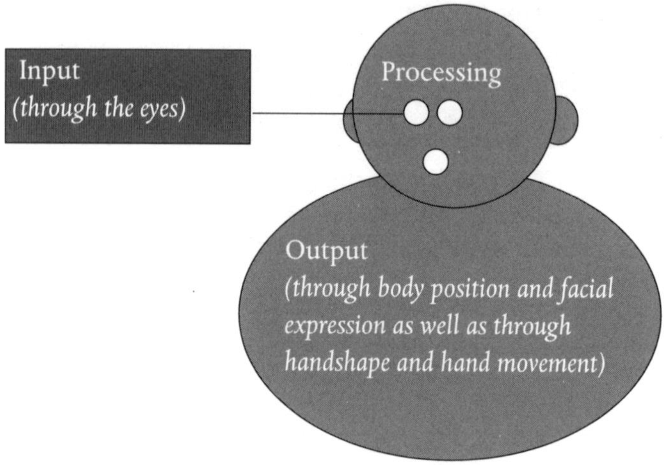

In this section then, we have looked at some of the factors that need to be taken into consideration when first grasping the concept of language processing. I have attempted to keep these factors evenly balanced by including reference to sign languages in all instances. This has not been in any way a natural tendency in linguistic research. It is only fairly recently that some linguists have realised that the study of sign language processing can reveal a great deal about spoken languages.

It is my personal view that we have yet to perceive how the body of linguistic research in general has been subconsciously influenced and weighted in favour of an oral/aural modality of language. I am certain that, in time, sign language research will enable researchers to throw considerable light on the nature of language universals. We have now seen that language acquisition, language production and language perception occur naturally for both signed and spoken languages provided that the appropriate conditions for access of input data (samples of the language) are met (Chamberlain, Morford and Mayberry 2000).

Are words and signs related?

Now we will look at some examples[2] of how the actual performances of signed and spoken languages differ, using English and Irish sign Language (ISL), and see if it is possible to draw some general conclusions about whether the processing systems involved have common factors. We will first take examples of nouns, adjectives and pronouns. Then we will look at plurality and word order in both languages. Finally we will identify some grammatical elements of ISL (also present in other sign languages) that are not present in English

Nouns and adjectives

Are words and signs interchangeable? People often ask what is the sign for such and such a word. Sometimes it is relatively easy to answer, for example with generic forms of words and signs like 'book' or 'table.' The ISL glosses for these words are BOOK and TABLE respectively.

ILLUSTRATION 1: BOOK

More often, it is necessary to ask what the context is of what it is you wish to say since a lot more additional information can be incorporated (inflected) into a sign in ISL than into a word in English. For example the dimensions of the book or the table can be incorporated into the noun by the use of classifier handshapes (see Matthews 1996 and O'Baoill 2000). Very often it is necessary to ask what context the word is being used in so that the exact noun can be conveyed by the classifier handshape.

ILLUSTRATION 2: OPEN

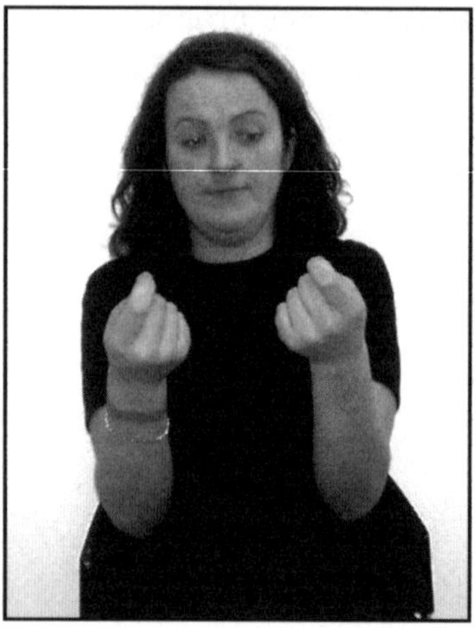

CL thin entity

OPEN

The use of a classifier handshape, for example 'thin entity' will allow a number of different interpretations of the noun. 'I opened a birthday card' and 'I opened a magazine' will look exactly the same but context will allow the correct interpretation.

ILLUSTRATION 3: OPEN

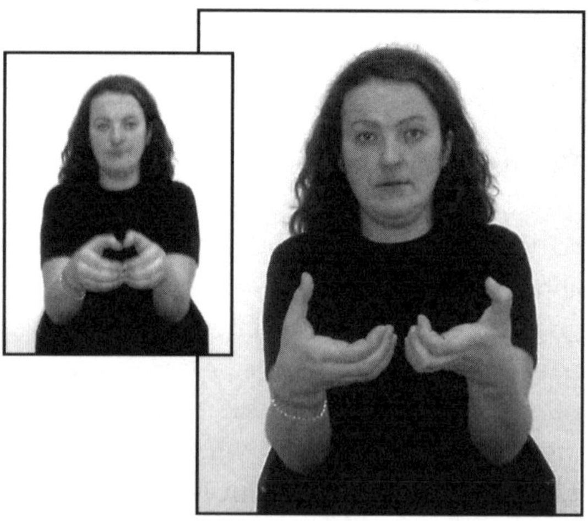

CL thick entity

OPEN

'I opened a thick book'

In English we must use additional, separate words with the noun to convey adjectival information such as 'thick' or 'rectangular.' The ISL example here uses the classifier handshape for 'thick entity.'

The really interesting linguistic difference in these particular examples is that ISL can sometimes convey a certain amount of linguistic information more quickly than English can as, effectively, two items of information can be delivered at the same time. It is this simultaneous aspect of sign language that makes it unique. It is literally impossible to say two words at the same time. Sometimes a significant amount of information can be given in a sign language more quickly than it can be said.

One study found that speaking rate was twice as quick as signing rate (Bellugi and Fisher 1972, cited in Tartter 1998b) but this trial was of storytelling in speech and sign and the subjects were allowed to tell the stories in their own words, so general conclusions can not be drawn. In a further study the number of propositions were counted rather than the number of signs or words and under this analysis similar rates of production were apparent for both modes.

Plurality

The following examples from English give two phrases demonstrating plurality: '-s' (one of the English grammatical morphemes for plurality) is added to the word 'tree' to give the plural form, and the additional nouns 'forest' and 'avenue' give the context.

The ISL sign for 'tree' can be 'inflected' to include additional information in respect of number. The movement of the handshape for TREE, drawn in space, mirrors the line of trees in the tree-lined avenue it represents. In ISL, the sign for TREE is inflected for number by the ISL grammatical morpheme for plurality which means that the sign for a single tree is extended or repeated. In illustration 5 the trees are shown to be in a line and in illustration 6 they are shown as randomly placed.

ILLUSTRATION 4: TREE

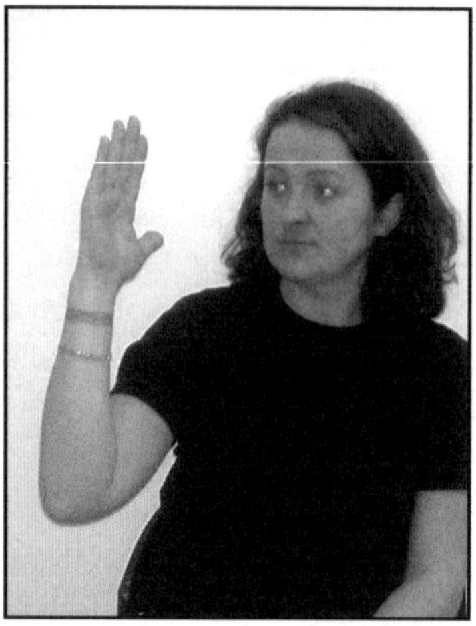

TREE

ILLUSTRATION 5: TREE

TREE++++++++++++++++++++++++(RH)

'One side of the road was lined with trees'

ILLUSTRATION 6: TREE

TREE++++++(RH/LH)
'There was a forest'

The examples shown in illustrations 5 and 6 can be translated into English as 'avenue of trees', 'forest of trees' or even 'dense forest of trees.'

A different type of example of plural can be seen in 'parked cars' (see overleaf). The same morph of reduplication is used to demonstrate 'parked', but this time the generic sign for car is replaced by the classifier handshape for VEHICLE. The VEHICLE classifier handshape is used to indicate the number and manner of the parked vehicles. With slight modifications to the placing of the 'vehicle' classifier handshape, the cars can be shown to be parked in rows, in a single line, or randomly. Again, it is not possible to find individual lexical equivalents in English that match the individual signs; instead additional words must be sought to capture a similar meaning.

ILLUSTRATION 7: CAR

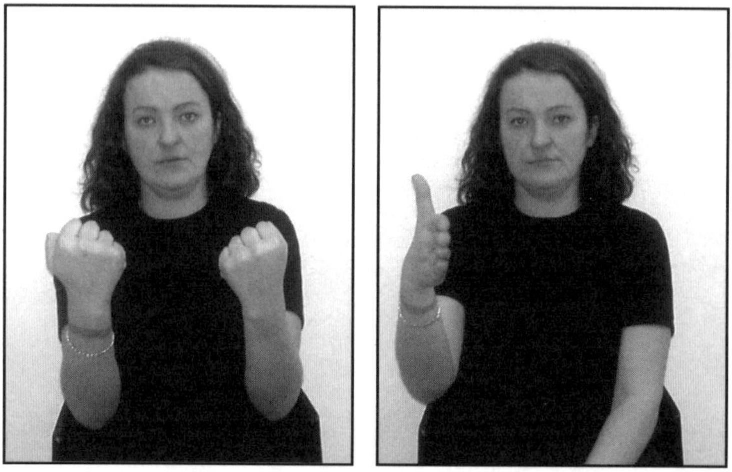

CL VEHICLE

CAR

ILLUSTRATION 8: CAR PARKED

CAR PARKED

'The car was parked'

ILLUSTRATION 9: CARS PARKED

<u>CL VEHICLE</u>

CARS PARKED

'The cars were parked in a line' (as along the road)

ILLUSTRATION 10: CARS PARKED

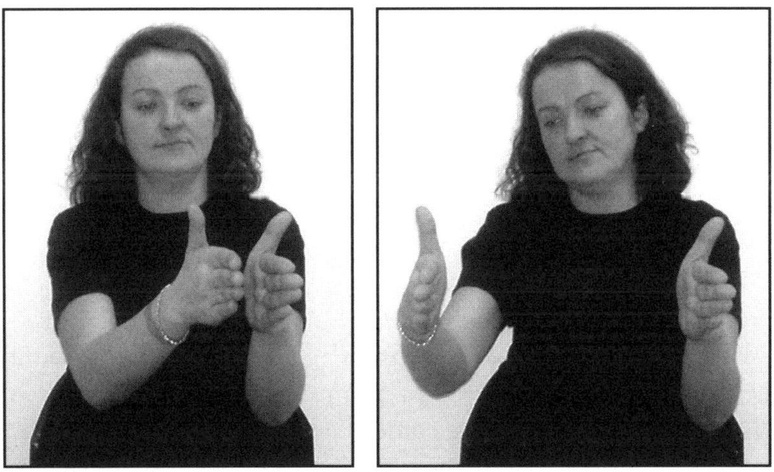

<u>CL VEHICLE</u>

CARS PARKED

'The cars were parked in rows' (as in a car park)

ILLUSTRATION 11: CARS PARKED

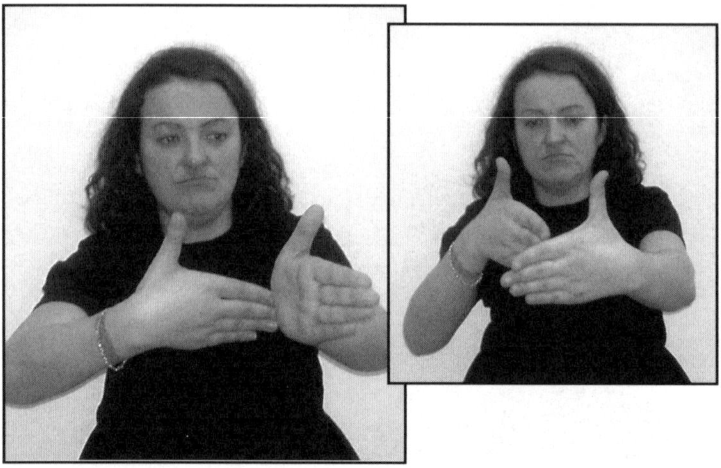

CL VEHICLE

CARS PARKED

'The cars were parked randomly'

Pronouns

Another area where ISL and English linguistic performances are radically different is that of pronominal reference or pronouns. The English pronouns employ a separate word for each possibility of reference allowed by the grammar: 'he', 'she', 'it', 'we', 'they', etc. In signed languages a contextually relevant index referent identifies the pronoun. The example in illustration 12 is called 'index reference.' The referent indicated by the pointing first finger can be 'he', 'she', or 'it' depending on the context. Illustration 13 shows that ISL allows constructions that English does not have.

Examples such as these would translate as 'the two of us', 'we three', 'the three of them', 'the four of them', 'groups of three/four/five'... Again, the interpretation is context dependent as when oneself is included in a group of three: 'we three' as opposed to 'the three of you', for example.

ILLUSTRATION 12: INDEX REFERENT (SINGULAR)

YOU

ILLUSTRATION 13: INDEX REFERENT (PLURAL)
WE TWO / THE FOUR OF YOU

WE TWO

THE FOUR OF YOU

Word and sign strings (syntax)

The order in which we say or sign something is also important. The two examples below are not the only way of expressing this situation, but they are both acceptable and grammatical in their respective languages.

English A dog sat on my red hat.
ISL gloss RED HAT MINE THERE d-o-g WALK WALK WALK [classifier] SIT-ON-TOP-OF-HAT [classifier]

The following example is not grammatical in English because it has incorrect word order:

English * Dog my red hat sat on a.

Similar ungrammatical examples can be generated in ISL that also demonstrate that the order of the elements is critical. The second of the two examples below shows an unacceptable sentence in English. The wrong morph has been attached to the root 'happy', '-ily' is the adverbial ending and '-ness' is the noun ending.

English 1. Susan skipped happily to the park.
*2. Susan skipped happiness to the park.

As native speakers/signers we don't make these kinds of 'mistakes' and generally we know if a sentence sounds or looks right. A mistake like this could not occur in ISL because the form of the sign HAPPY is determined by the context in which it is signed. In the following example it will be perfectly obvious that the manner of Susan's skipping is 'happy' from the inflection of the verb and the accompanying non manual features (NMF's).

NMF adverbial 'happy'
ISL gloss PARK THERE SUSAN SKIP SKIP SKIP

In English, verbs can be marked for time and number so they may also give information about when the action happened and who initiated it. In the next example we consider the way children unknowingly learn the irregular past tense of the first person singular of the English verb 'to go'.

English * I goed to the shops.
I went to the shops.

The child has acquired the regular past tense ending of -ed for verbs such as 'walk', 'cook', 'talk', but has not yet realised that some verbs are irregular (Ingram 1989). Studies show that deaf children acquire language in exactly the same developmental stages as hearing children (Chamberlain *et al* 2000). Again, this is a mistake that would not occur in ISL discourse. In ISL, time may be indicated by a time marker such as YESTERDAY or FINISH before the events were relayed, and subsequent verbs are assumed to refer to the past until a new time marker is set in the discourse (Leeson 1996).

ILLUSTRATION 14: SHOPPING FINISH

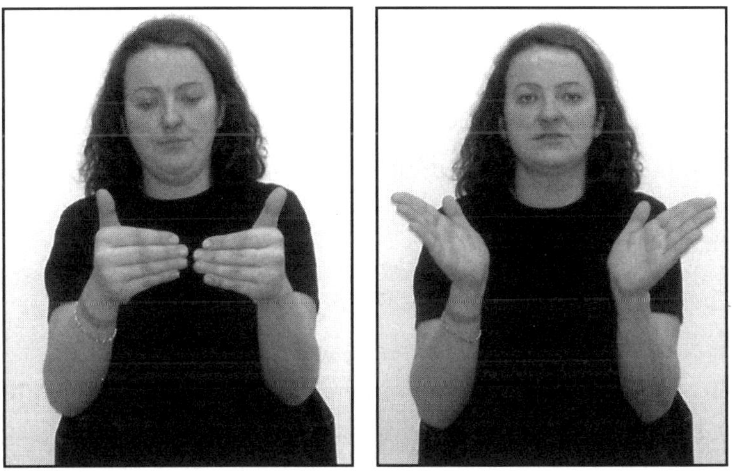

SHOPPING FINISH
'I went shopping.'

Rules control our language behaviours

All the above examples go to prove Chomsky's hypothesis that linguistic communication operates under a system of rules, and that the rules are different for each language. We can say that all languages are thus constrained and therefore that all language processing systems are similar in so much as they use 'constraints' or rules that native users have covert knowledge of, that is, they have a functioning grammar at a subconscious level and can use the language correctly and observe when errors are present in the discourse of others. It is the common acquisition of functioning grammar that allows us to be mutually intelligible.

The system of rules that govern language processing is commonly known as a grammar. Both ISL and English have their own grammars, grammars that are suited to their respective modes, but which still express grammatical forms such as nouns, verbs, adjectives and adverbs, pronouns and time marking. Anyone who has studied another spoken language will have come to realise some of these rules consciously, and indeed much of second language learning will centre on mastering them. In trying to make sense of the nonsense sentence below we will take *grack* to be a verb and *splab* to be a noun because we are used to this construction, even though we have no idea what they might mean.[3]

English I grack the splab.

Similarly, we can also identify an adverb, 'plobbly', because adverbs usually follow verbs and end in '–ly' and an adjective, 'troxious', because adjectives usually precede nouns and '-ious' is known to us as an adjectival morph.

English I grack plobbly the troxious splab.

The reason we have to learn grammar when we learn a second language is to allow us to consciously construct sentences as opposed to our natural (subconscious) constructions in our primary languages. Language processing therefore knows that languages behave in this manner and can produce, for example, a question form in English by using WH words (what, who, when, where) and by using a question marker (raised eyebrows) in ISL.

Non-manual features in ISL (and in other sign languages) are a modality discrete feature of sign languages. This means they are only found in visio-spatial languages. The ability to articulate two linguistic items at the same time in a compound is also a modality effect of visio-spatial language as is the ability to describe events simultaneously. We can describe all these differences in the performance of the features of English and ISL grammars as being modality discrete. Language pro-

ILLUSTRATION 15: TEXT PHONE

TEXT PHONE

ILLUSTRATION 16: DRIVE-CAR (AND) TALK-ON-PHONE

DRIVE ARE (AND) TALK-ON-PHONE
'As I was driving the car I was also speaking on the mobile phone.'

cessing therefore is most similar in its cognitive elements and most different in its physical elements. It seems to be of no consequence whether a communication is spoken or signed as long as the transfer from the cognitive construction of a communication act to its physical articulation is in line with a grammar that is appropriate to the modality of the utterance. The general view of sign language researchers is that there are more similarities than differences in spoken and signed language processing:

> Processing of sign generally manifests more similarities to processing of speech than differences' (Tartter 1998b:189);
>
> Thus we can see from these studies that despite great differences in surface form, signed and spoken languages use at least some of the same processing mechanisms in resolving and interpreting co-reference relations (Emmorey 1997:118);
>
> ...the formal role of distinctive features, syllables, and segments as building blocks of a grammar with constraints is the same for signed and spoken languages but [...] the substantive definitions in both types of languages—those that are more phonetic and less grammatical—depend on conditions of naturalness in each modality and on specifics about production and processing that grow out of experiences with linguistic messages conveyed in each (Brentari 1998:313).

In this section, by discussing some glossed examples of ISL and some examples of written English, I have shown that there are vast differences between the performances of the two languages. It appears that word and sign performance of noun and adjective forms use different structures to convey similar amounts of linguistic information. This has also shown to be true for word and sign order, pronouns, and time marking.

We have also seen that there are things one can do with spoken languages that cannot be done with signed languages and visa versa. One of these is that whereas you may not speak or articulate two lexical entities at the same time, you can do so in sign. We can say that ISL has serial, temporal and simultaneous production options. This means that linguistic information in signs can be produced as one lexical item after another over a period of time (temporally and serially) and that lexical items can also be produced simultaneously. In the following example, the verb DRIVE is articulated with the left hand at the same time as the verb TALK-ON-PHONE is articulated with the right:

(I) DRIVE TALK-ON-PHONE
Translation: I was driving and talking on the phone

English only allows the production of linguistic information in terms of one lexical item after another over a period of time, that is, serially and temporally. It is this feature that has led to the past and present erroneous belief that ISL is a type of 'shorthand English.'

Conclusion

The question posed in the title of this paper, 'are words and signs related', has now been answered. By acknowledging that all languages operate under a system of rules called a grammar, by examining nouns, adjectives, pronouns, time marking, and by discussing some of the components of syntax (word/sign order), we have collated sufficient information and can see enough of an emerging pattern to answer the given question. Not too surprisingly, the answer is a 'yes and no' answer. It is clear that there are striking similarities between words and signs, that is, between English and ISL. Both languages have grammars, both are able to describe who initiated an action, give information about the action, and describe its effects on other people or things. Both languages can place discourse within a time frame and make pronominal substitution. In short, sign languages can achieve all the communicative outcomes that have been historically attributed to spoken languages. It is also clear, however, that behaviours associated with the articulation of words and signs do differ.

As has been shown, signs function as well as words at a deep level of structure in mental processing. It is at this level of cognitive structure that the rules that form the grammars of both languages operate and it is here that both languages are most similar. However, as the modality of each language is different, the results of that processing which manifest in the physical world, that is, words or signs, are vastly different in form. We can conclude, therefore, by saying that signs and words are closely linked at the level of formulation but not at all closely linked at the level of performance.

The incorporation of signed languages into the body of current and future linguistic theory and research will not only present a view of language in its broadest and most accurate sense, but will hopefully also be the means of preventing misunderstandings and misperceptions about deaf infants, deaf children, and deaf people that will allow both appropriate early intervention strategies and appropriate future curricula to be developed at all levels of society and education for deaf children and people.

Notes

1. I will not speculate here on to what extent a taste, smell or touch mode of language might exist, but mention the possibility only in the context of linguistic input and output data requirements for sensory channels to bridge cognitive and real world performances.
2. All glossed ISL examples have been taken from direct observation of native signers and are used with permission.
   I would like to thank Carmel Grehan for her input and examples of ISL lexical items.
3. Edward Lear's nonsense poem makes use of this fact.

References

Baddeley, A. (1997) *Human Memory, Theory and Practice (Revised Edition)*, Hove, UK: Psychology Press.

Chamberlain, C., Morford, J.P. and Mayberry, R.I. (2000) *Language Acquisition by Eye*, London: Lawrence Erlbaum Associates.

Chomsky, N. (1986) *Knowledge of Language: Its Nature, Origins and Use*, New York: Praeger.

Crystal, D. (4th ed.) (1997) *A Dictionary of Linguistics and Phonetics*, Oxford: Blackwell.

Duffin, D. (forthcoming) Unpublished post-graduate research on appropriate curricula, Centre for Language and Communication Studies, University of Dublin, Trinity College.

—— (1998) *The Effects of Modality Difference on Cognitive and Linguistic Development*, Unpublished M.Phil. dissertation, University of Dublin, Trinity College.

—— (1999) Deafness and Language Acquisition, *Teanga*, 18:93–105.

Emmorey, K. (1997) Non-Antecendent Suppression in American Sign Language, *Language and Cognitive Processes*, 12(1):103–119.

—— (2002) *Language, Cognition and the Brain: Insights from Sigh Language*, London: Lawrence Erlbaum Associates.

Groce, N. E. (1985) *Everyone Here Spoke Sign Language*, Cambridge Mass.: Harvard University Press.

Harley, T. (2001) *The Psychology of Language: From Data to Theory*, Hove, UK: Psychology Press

Ingram, D (1989) *first Language Acquisition: Method Description and Explanation*, Cambridge: Cambridge University Press.

Leeson, L. (1996) *The Expression of Time in Sign Language with Special Reference to ISL*, Unpublished M.Phil. dissertation, University of Dublin, Trinity College.

Matthews, P. (1996) Extending the Lexicon of Irish Sign Language, The Irish Yearbook of Applied Linguistics, *Teanga*, 16: 135–167.

O'Baoill, D. and Matthews, P. (2000) *The Irish Deaf Community: The Structure of Irish Sign Language, Vol. 2*, Dublin: Institiúid Teangeolaíochta Éireann.

Stokoe, W. (1960) Sign Language Structure: An Outline of the Visual Communications Systems of the American Deaf, *Studies in Linguistics: Occasional Papers 8*, Silver Spring, MD: Linstok Press.

Tartter, V. C. (1998a) *Language and its Normal Processing*, London: Sage Publications.

—— (1998b) *Language Processing in Atypical Populations*, London: Sage Publications.

An introduction to verb categories in Irish Sign Language

Patrick McDonnell

Introduction

Verbs seem to be an essential feature of all human languages. It is difficult to imagine how a language could work without them. Verbs have a central role in modern theories of grammar because they have the capacity to link with other important parts of a sentence. When we analyse verbs we can learn a lot about the structure of a language itself. Some linguists have used the relationship between the verb (V), the subject (S) and the object (O) to classify languages. In this classification there are six possible language types—SVO, SOV, VSO, VOS, OVS and OSV (Greenberg 1966). SVO languages like English and SOV languages like Japanese together make up 75% of the world's languages, and VSO languages like Irish make up a further 15% (Crystal 1987:98). Languages which place the object first (OVS and OSV) are rare but a group of these languages has been found in the Amazon basin.

Another important class of languages should also be mentioned—TC or Topic Comment languages. In comparison with English, some sign languages—like Irish Sign Language (ISL)—seem to favour a TC structure. Of course when we note that English is a SVO language or that ISL favours TC utterances, it means that these are typical structures in that language, not that they are the only structures.

Categorising verbs

It is possible to group verbs in different ways. In a semantic grouping, for example, verbs would be categorised according to their meaning. Verbs of emotion and feeling (HATE, LOVE, BE-SORRY) could be placed in one category, verbs of physical action (WALK, RUN, SWIM) in another category, and verbs of mental activity (KNOW, THINK, REMEMBER) in further category.

A more common practice is to group verbs in terms of their morphology. In morphology we look at the form of the verb and analyse the details of its structure. Where is the onset or beginning point of the sign? Where is the offset or end point? Do the onset or offset locations have any meaning in themselves? How does the hand move? Does the form of the verb change or stay the same in different syntactic contexts? Does the handshape by itself have a separate meaning?

In analysing verbs in ISL it is necessary refer to the following terms: agreement, person, motion, movement, classifier, locus and locus marker. 'Agreement' means that some part of the verb structure is linked to or agrees with some other element in a sentence. 'Person' is a grammatical term which is used to distinguish between the sender, the receiver, or a third party in relation to a message. PRON-c (I/ME) refers to the first person (that is, the sender of a message); PRON-f, PRON-fr, etc. (YOU, SHE, etc.) refers to a non-first person (such as the receiver). Notation terms such as 'c', 'f' and 'fr' are explained in section 3, below.

The term 'motion' denotes that some person or thing moves from one location to another while 'movement' is used to refer to movement of the hand(s) as a sign is being articulated. 'Classifier' (CL) means that a handshape in itself has a particular meaning. For example, Index-CL (the 'D' hand in ISL) refers to a human or human-like entity; Multiple entity-CL (the 'claw' hand) refers to a large number of entities such as a crowd; Small round entity-CL (the flat 'O' hand) refers to an object like a nut or small stone. The term CL is included in the notation to show that the handshape has this particular or separate meaning. Not all handshapes have such a meaning; for example, the handshapes used in PLAY or NO do not have any special meaning.

Locus and locus markers in sign languages

Two further terms should be mentioned: 'locus' (pl. loci) and 'locus marker'. A locus refers to a particular location in signing space. It is an abstract entity. Although we cannot actually 'see' a locus, its presence and location are indicated by a locus marker. Locus markers are shown by the position and/or orientation of the hand(s). Example (1) illustrates locus and locus marker features:

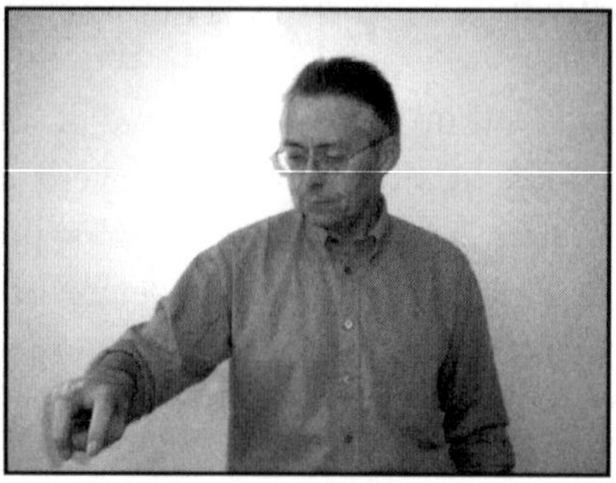

(1) HOUSE-fr BOY V-CL+MOVE+fr
'The boy went to the house.'

When the sign HOUSE in (1) is made the hands are placed in a forward-right (fr) position. This position marks the location of HOUSE in signing space and we refer to this special location as a locus. HOUSE is now related to or is 'at' this forward-right locus. When the sign V-CL+MOVE is made the hand moves outward in a forward-right direction. The hand must also be oriented in the same forward-right direction. Together, the orientation and offset (final) position of the hand in the sign V-CL+MOVE make up the locus marker which indicates the locus 'fr.'

We already know that HOUSE is 'at' the locus 'fr' so the sign V-CL+MOVE +fr with its own locus marker indicates the same locus. And if we want to 'look at' the house or 'see' the house, the form of the verb LOOK-AT or SEE must include the correct locus marker (that is, LOOK-AT+fr and SEE+fr). There are many possible loci in signing space. The most common loci on a horizontal plane are as follows:

f
fl fr
sl c sr
Signer

The most common loci on a vertical plane are:

hi
Signer c f
lo

In Irish Sign Language a locus can refer to a person or a place. The 'c' locus is sometimes called the sender locus and refers to the 'first person' (I/ME) or to 'this location' (HERE). The other loci refer to a 'non-first person' (YOU/SHE/IT/ etc.) or to 'that location' (THERE).

Researchers in several sign languages have identified three characteristic verb groups: agreement, plain and classifier. Although different researchers have used different terms to label these categories, the terms agreement, plain and classifier are widely recognised. For analysis and discussion of verbs in other sign languages see Brennan (1992) and Sutton-Spence and Woll (1999) for British Sign Language; Padden (1990) and Valli and Lucas (1992) for American Sign Language; Engberg-Pedersen (1993) for Danish Sign Language. Researchers have also identified sub-categories within these three main groups. For the purposes of this paper, however, we will focus on the distinctive features of these three general categories of verbs in ISL. A more detailed analysis of verbs in ISL may be found in McDonnell (1996) and Leeson (2001).

Agreement verbs

We will begin with agreement verbs because it is relatively easy to compare and contrast agreement verbs with other types of verbs. Agreement verbs in ISL always incorporate one or two locus markers. These verbs are called agreement verbs because their locus markers are linked to or agree with some noun or pronoun in the sentence. Because these locus markers agree with a noun or pronoun they are usually referred to as agreement markers. Here are two examples of agreement, one from ISL (2) and one from English (3):

In (2), the verb ACCUSE agrees with ALL CLASS and with 'first person' (i.e. the signer). The locus markers are indicated by the orientation of the hands: the marker 'f' shows agreement with ALL CLASS and the marker 'c' shows agreement with 'first person'. ACCUSE is an agreement verb because it can accept such agreement markers. In (3), the verb 'likes' agrees with 'cat.' The 's' in 'likes' is the marker that shows agreement with 'cat' (overleaf). Further examples of agreement verbs in ISL are shown in examples (4)–(7).

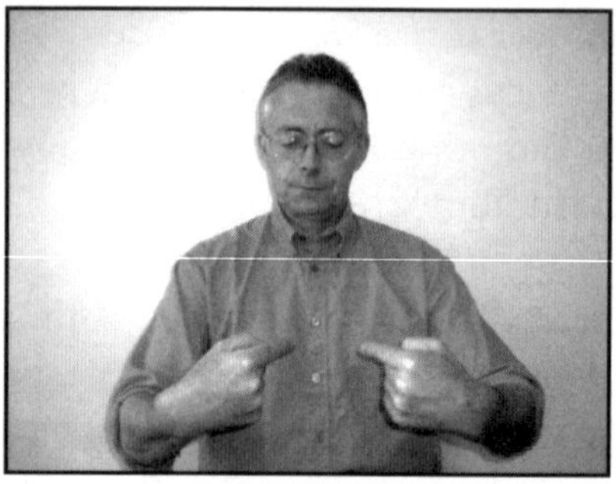

(2) ALL CLASS f+ACCUSE+c
'The whole class blamed me.'

(3) The cat likes milk

(4) TV-fl BOY c+IGNORE+fl TV-fl
'The boy ignored the television.'

(5) PRIEST BE-THERE+f PRON-c c+GET-ATTENTION-OF+f
'The priest was there and I button-holed him.'

(6) BOY fr+CARRY-BY-HAND+c FOOD
(Literally: The boy carried food from there to here.)
The boy brought in food.

(7) BOY hi / c+RUN+lo / f
(Literally: The boy ran from up here to down there.)
The boy ran downstairs.

The verbs in those examples are all agreement verbs. Each verb has two locus markers which function as agreement markers. The referents of the markers in (4) and (5) are somewhat different from the referents of the markers in (6) and (7). The markers in (4) and (5) agree with 'person' referents (the Subject or Object of the verb); the markers in (6) and (7) agree with 'location' referents (the Source or Goal of the verb). Thus, in ISL there are two kinds of agreement verbs: person agreement verbs and locative agreement verbs. Verbs like GET-ATTENTION-OF and IGNORE are person agreement verbs because their markers agree with 'person' referents. Verbs such as CARRY-BY-HAND and RUN are locative agreement verbs because their markers agree with 'location' referents.

Plain verbs

Plain verbs do not accept agreement markers. The form of a plain verb normally remains the same even when other elements in the sentence are changed or when the verb is used in a different syntactic context. In the following examples, (8) and (9), the form of the verb REMEMBER is the same in both sentences although the subject and object are reversed.

(8) ALL CLASS REMEMBER PRON-C
'The whole class remembered me.'

(9) PRON-C REMEMBER ALL CLASS
'I remembered all the class.'

REMEMBER has no markers to show agreement with its subject or object. Many plain verbs are 'body-anchored' signs, the same as REMEMBER. 'Body-anchored' means that the articulation of the sign involves touching, or almost touching, some part of the body. The following plain verbs involve body contact:

LIKE, LOVE, HATE, BE-ANGRY, BE-INTERESTED, BE-SHOCKED, FEEL, THINK, KNOW, UNDERSTAND, LIE.

Other plain verbs do not involve body contact; in these, the sign is articulated at or near some part of the body. The following are some examples:

FORGET, KILL, PUNISH, DE-DISAPPOINTED, LAUGH, EAT, DRINK, BE-LARGE, FINISH, BE-BOLD, BE-ASHAMED.

This 'body-anchored' structure makes it impossible or unlikely for these signs to incorporate agreement markers. Sometimes, however, the movement in a plain verb may look like an agreement marker. A good example is the verb RESPECT. When the sign RESPECT is articulated the hands move outward from the body (10). Do the onset (beginning) and offset (end) positions of the hands indicate agreement markers?

(10) PRON-c RESPECT PRON-f
'I respect you.'

It is possible to conduct a test to establish whether the onset and offset positions of the hands in RESPECT are agreement markers or not. In the test, the subject and the object positions in the sentence are reversed, as shown in examples (10) and (11). If the onset and offset positions of RESPECT in (11) are not allowed to change and remain the same as in (10), then the verb is not allowed to accept agreement markers. If, however, the onset and offset positions of the sign are allowed to change, then these positions must be agreement markers.

(11) PRON-f RESPECT PRON-c
'You respect me.'

In (11) the movement and positioning of the hands in RESPECT are the same as in (10), and example (11) is an acceptable sentence. But what happens if we try to add agreement markers to RESPECT, with the onset position at 'f' and the offset position at 'c', as in (12)?

(12) * PRON-f f+RESPECT+c PRON-c
'You respect me.'

 Example (12) an ungrammatical sentence. Therefore, the onset and offset positions in RESPECT are not agreement markers and RESPECT must be considered to be a plain verb. Interestingly, in American Sign Language, both (10) and (12) are acceptable sentences. Thus, ASL has different grammatical rules than ISL; in ASL RESPECT is an agreement verb.

Classifier verbs

Classifier verbs are probably the most interesting and complex verbs in ISL. Although classifier verbs are a characteristic feature of sign languages there has been a lot of argument among researchers about them (Emmory, 2003). For example: Is 'classifier' the correct term for these verbs? What is their structure? What is the best way to analyse them?

Most researchers, however, agree that classifier verbs have two basic parts—a handshape and a movement. But almost every sign has a handshape and a movement. What makes the handshape and movement in classifier verbs different from the handshape and movement in other verb signs? The major difference is that in classifier verbs the handshape and the movement have special or additional meanings that are not found in other verb signs. For example, the handshape and movement in the verb in (13) have particular meanings, while the handshape and movement in the verb in (14) do not have any separate or particular meanings.

(13) V-CL+C+MOVE-small vertical arc+f

Both handshape and movement have particular meanings.
Handshape: V-CL = two legs + animate entity
Movement: MOVE = an arcing motion in the real world
(Literally: A two-legged animate entity moved in this way from here to there.)
Someone went up and over.

(14) RESPECT
Neither the handshape and movement have any separate meanings.
Handshape: R = Ø (zero value)
Movement: an outward arc from the signer = Ø
'respect'

Handshapes in classifier verbs

There are many classifier handshapes in ISL. However, we can include all these handshapes under three general headings—whole entity handshapes, handle entity handshapes and extension handshapes. In the first group, the handshapes represent a whole entity (Whole entity-CL). Sentence (15) is an example. In this example, the handshape V-CL refers to the whole person, not just the legs. A whole entity handshape may tell us how many dimensions an entity has: 0-dimensional, 1-dimensional, 2-dimensional, or 3-dimensional. It may also indicate the general shape or contour of the entity: straight, curved, angled, circular, flat, and so on.

(15) HOUSE-fr BOY V-CL+MOVE+fr
The boy went to the house.

In the second group, handle entity, the handshape does not represent the entity itself. Instead it expresses the shape of the hand as it moves, uses or touches an entity. Examples are: Handle entity-CL ('A' hand), Handle small entity-CL (modified 'G' hand), Handle flat entity-CL (modified 'B' hand). In example (16) below, the signer uses two hands to indicate how an entity was handled. The dominant hand shows how the RADIO was held. The subordinate hand shows how it was supported underneath.

(16) PRIEST Handle entity-CL+sr+MOVE+f ----- RADIO
Handle flat surface-CL+sr+MOVE+f
'The priest carried in a radio.'

In the third group, extension handshapes, the hands are used to trace the shape and/or size of an entity. Examples of Extension-CL verbs are: Trace rectangular entity-CL ('D' hand), Trace narrow entity (modified 'G' hand), or Trace flat surface entity-CL ('L' hand), as in example (17).

(17) SNOW Trace flat surface entity-CL+sl+EXTEND-large arc+fr
Flat surface entity-CL+sl+EXTEND --------------------
'The snow lay all about.'

In some classifier verbs the signer's body can function like a handshape. Therefore, the body classifier (Body-CL) can be included as a fourth member of this group, although it is not a handshape. Compare examples (18) and (19). In (18), the signer uses two hands to express a classifier verb construction. In example (19), the signer uses one hand and his body to express another classifier verb construction.

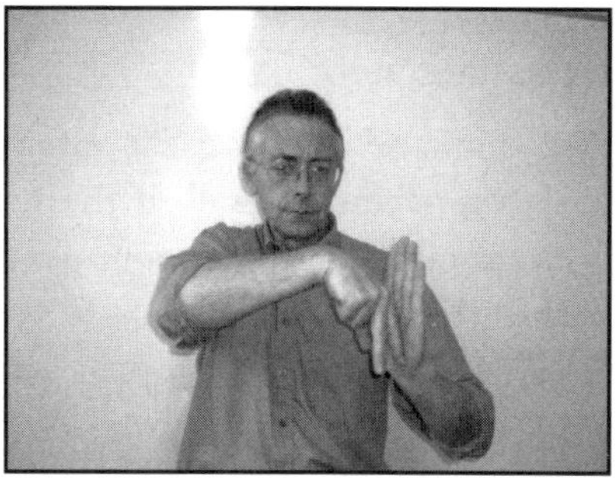

(18) WALL V-CL+BE-LOCATED+at left hand
vertical 2D entity-CL+EXIST ---
'Someone stood by the wall.'

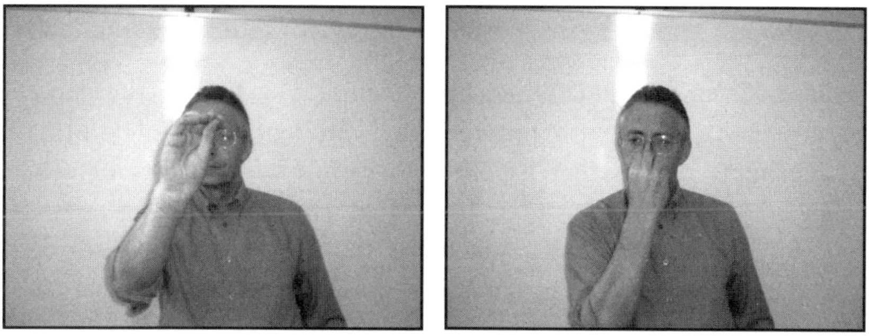

(19) SNOW^MAN THERE+f BOY handle small entity-CL+BE-LOCATED+f/hi
Handle small round entity-CL+BE-LOCATED+c
body-CL+EXIST+nose -----------------------------
'The boy gave the snowman a nose.'

In (19) the signer uses a flat O handshape (Handle small entity-CL) in articulating the verb. The signer first moves his hand to a locus 'f' at face height. This locus agrees with the noun SNOW^MAN which has been located at 'f.' Then the signer moves his hand towards himself. His hand stops just in front of his nose. We know that the locus is 'nose' because the signer does not move his body. So in (19) the signer's body has the same function as the subordinate hand in (18).

Movements in classifier verbs

When classifier verbs are articulated, the hand(s) may make different kinds of movements, or may make no movement at all. If the hand does not move, a zero movement value is given. There are four general kinds of movement in classifier verbs. These are MOVE, BE-LOCATED, EXIST (zero movement) and EXTEND. MOVE is articulated by an actual movement of the hand(s) in signing space. The term MOVE provides two different kinds of information. It can denote how an entity moves from one place to another by itself or how someone moves something. The meaning depends on which handshape MOVE combines with:

Whole entity-CL+MOVE = Something moves by itself (15);
Handle entity-CL+MOVE = Someone moves something (16).

BE-LOCATED is characterised by a 'stamping' action of the hand. The term BE-LOCATED also provides two different kinds of information, depending on whether it combines with a whole entity or a handle entity handshape. It can indicate that an entity (such as a person) is located in a particular place ('by the wall' in example 18) or that someone has put an entity ('nose') in a particular place ('where a nose should be' in example 19).

(18) WALL V-CL+BE-LOCATED+by left hand
Vertical 2D entity-CL+EXIST ------
'Someone stood by the wall.'

(19) SNOW^MAN THERE+f BOY Handle small entity-CL+BE-LOCATED+f/hi
Handle small round entity-CL+BE-LOCATED+c
Body-CL+EXIST+nose ----------------------------
'The boy gave the snowman a nose.'

Zero movement denotes EXIST. EXIST is used when we want to show that an entity is present but we are not concerned about its exact location. There is no stamping movement by the hand. In (19) above, the signer's body is 'present' so the verb may be described as Body-CL+EXIST. Another example is shown in (20).

(20) Cylindrical entity-CL+EXIST+fr g-l-a-s-s
'There was a glass there…'

The final kind of movement is EXTEND. In EXTEND the movement of the hand does not refer to the movement of the entity in question. Instead, the movement of the hand 'draws' the shape or size of the entity in signing space. EXTEND movements can combine only with Extension-CL handshapes. Examples are (21) and (22).

(21) SNOW Trace flat surface entity-CL+sl+EXTEND-large arc+fr
Flat surface entity-CL+sl+EXTEND --------------------
'The snow lay all about.'

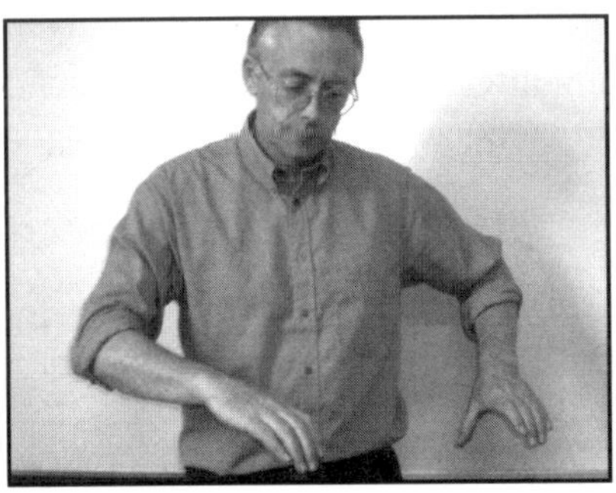

(22) ICE f-r-e-e-z-e-r Trace long 3D entity-CL+EXTEND+fr
Trace long 3D entity-CL+EXTEND+sl
'There was a chest freezer…'

Handshape and movement categories

We can now summarise in a diagram how the different handshapes and movements combine with one another and which particular combinations are acceptable.

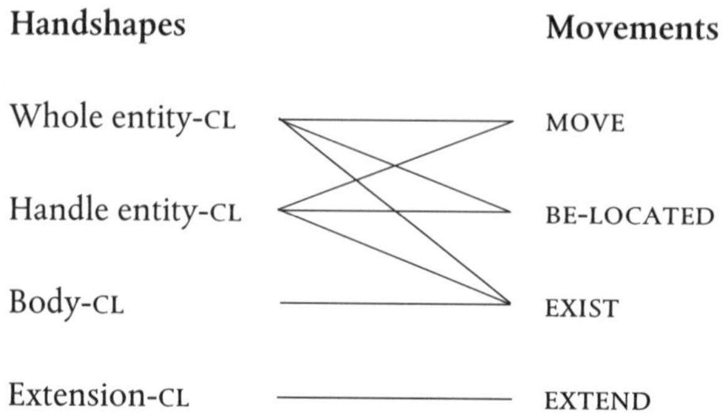

Conclusion

This chapter has described three different groups of verbs in ISL. We can recognise agreement verbs because they accept and incorporate agreement markers. We saw that some agreement verbs agree with 'person' while others agree with 'location'. The main difference between these sub-groups is found in the nature of the arguments that control agreement. Animacy is an important feature of the arguments that control agreement in person agreement verbs while locative agreement verbs typically occur in contexts which express spatial relations between the verb and its arguments.

Plain verbs tend to have a characteristic 'body anchored' structure and differ from agreement verbs because they do not accept agreement markers. Plain verbs also differ from classifier verbs because the handshape in a plain verb does not have any particular or separate meaning.

We recognise classifier verbs because their handshapes and movements (including zero movement) have special meanings. Classifier verbs share some of the features of locative agreement verbs. For example, Whole entity-CL and Handle entity-CL verbs can accept agreement markers for location. However, the handshape in agreement verbs does not indicate a particular meaning. One exception to this rule is the verb GIVE which appears to be a typical agreement verb but in which the handshape may change according to the nature of the entity being given.[1] The following diagram summarises the major distinctions and relationships between verbs in ISL:

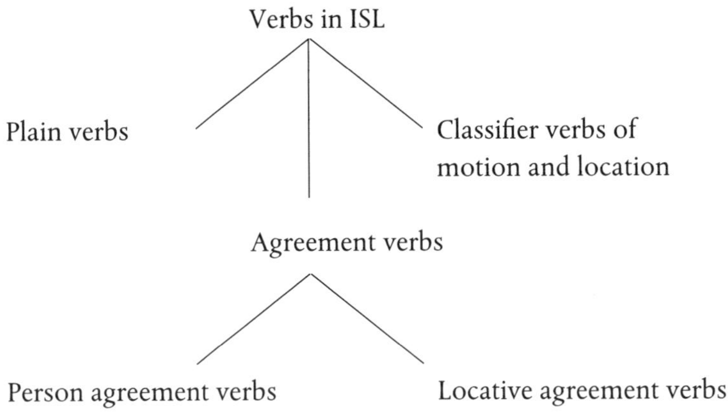

Note

1 A possible analysis here is to distinguish between two different verbs in ISL—GIVE and HAND-TO. GIVE is indicated only when the 'citation' handshape is used and is a classic agreement verb; HAND-TO is a classifier verb in which variable handshapes, indicating particular meanings, are used (Woll, personal communication).

Selected References

Baker, C. and Cokely, D. (1980) *American Sign Language: A Teacher's Resource Text on Grammar and Culture*, Silver Spring, Md.: T.J. Publishers.

Brennan, M. (1992) Introduction, in D. Brien (ed.) *Dictionary of British Sign Language / English*, London: Faber and Faber.

Crystal, D. (1987) *The Cambridge Encyclopedia of Language*, Cambridge: Cambridge University Press.

Emmory, K. (ed.) (2003) *Perspectives on Classifier Constructions in Sign Languages*, Mahwah, NJ: Lawrence Erlbaum Associates.

Engberg-Pedersen, E. (1993) *Space in Danish Sign Language: The Semantics and Morphosyntax of the Use of Space in a Visual Language*, Hamburg: Signum.

Greenberg, J. (1966, 2nd ed.) *Universals of Language*, Mouton: The Hague.

Kyle, J. and Woll, B. (1985) *Sign Language: The Study of Deaf People and their Language*, Cambridge: Cambridge University Press.

Leeson, L. (2001) *Aspects of Verbal Valency in Irish Sign Language*, unpublished PhD Thesis, University of Dublin, Trinity College.

Matthews, P. (1996) Extending the lexicon of Irish Sign Language, *Teanga*, Dublin: ITE.

McDonnell, P. (1996) How snowmen move: Some aspects of lexical choice in Irish Sign Language, *Teanga*, Dublin: ITE.

McDonnell, P. (1996) *Verb Categories in Irish Sign Language*, unpublished PhD Thesis, University of Dublin, Trinity College.

O'Baoill, D. and Matthews, P. (2000) *The Irish Deaf Community: The Structure of Irish Sign Language, vol. 2*, Dublin: The Linguistics Institute of Ireland.

Padden, C. (1990) The relation between space and grammar in ASL morphology, in C. Lucas (ed.) *Sign Language Research: Theoretical Issues*, Washington DC: Gallaudet University Press.

Supalla, T. (1986) The classifier system in American Sign Language, in C. Craig (ed.) *Noun Classes and Categorisation*, Amsterdam: John Benjamin Publishing Co.

Sutton-Spence, R. and Woll, B. (1999) *The Linguistics of British Sign Language: An Introduction*, Cambridge: Cambridge University Press.

Valli, C. and Lucas, C. (1992) *Linguistics of American Sign Language: A Resource Text for ASL Users*, Washington DC: Gallaudet University Press.

Woll, B. (1996) Personal communication.

III PATHS FOR THE FUTURE

Bilingualism and deafness

Joe McDonnell

Introduction

In a general sense the existence of bilingualism and bilingual education as a phenomenon can be traced from the ancient world through the Renaissance to the modern world (Lewis 1981). For example, linguistic diversity was very much part of life in the U.S. during the 18th and 19th centuries with European immigrants arriving with their languages and Native American languages already established there. In addition, bilingual schools using German and English were set up during the second half of the 19th century. Closer to home, a form of bilingual education was initiated by the Irish Free State in 1922 and in Wales the establishment of the first Welsh-medium school occurred in 1939 (Baker 2002).

It is often forgotten that Deaf people have also been part of this bilingual world. Early historical texts refer to Deaf people using sign language (Woll 1990) and literacy in the majority language was always an important component of Deaf education. Why is it, then, that the bilingual-bicultural perspective on deafness only became recognised in the 1980s and 1990s? One explanation is that sign language was not recognised as a full language but often regarded as a manual code for spoken language. In addition, modern linguists defined language in purely vocal/aural terms (Bloomfield 1933). This situation began to change in the 1960s with the first research into sign languages by modern linguists (Stokoe 1960). In 1972 Stockholm University initiated research into Swedish Sign Language. The modern bilingual perspective on deafness got some formal recognition in 1981 when the Swedish Parliament recognised Swedish Sign Language as a language and Deaf people as a bilingual group who '...have to be fluent in their visual/gestural sign language and in the language that society surrounds them with, Swedish' (Swedish National Association for the Deaf 1991:5). In

1989 more initiatives were taken to put these policies into place. Money was allocated to train sign language interpreters and sign language teachers, and to provide in-service courses for teachers of the Deaf in sign language. There has been some progress in Ireland towards recognition that Deaf people use two languages in their daily lives. The training of interpreters and sign language tutors, the Model School for the Deaf Project, the Link-Up project to assist adult Deaf literacy and the setting up of the Centre for Deaf Studies all indicate progress.

Bilingual abilities: What are they?

In very general terms we can define bilingualism as having two languages. For Deaf people this generally means fluency in a sign language combined with skills in literacy and varying degrees of oracy (listening/lip-reading and speaking) in a spoken language. However, a Deaf person may also be fluent in two or more sign languages.

One distinction that is often made in the study of bilingualism is between (i) individual bilingualism and (ii) bilingualism in society. Individual bilingualism may refer to both the language skills or abilities a person possesses and the frequency with which the individual uses the languages. It is common for individuals to vary in their bilingual ability and their usage of two languages. For example, a person may have good skills in English and Irish but use English on a daily basis and Irish less frequently. Another person may use two languages frequently but is fluent in only one of the languages. Bilingualism as an individual characteristic is also important as it may refer to how two languages affect our thinking and mental activities.

An individual has to master four important skills in learning a spoken language. These abilities can be looked at across two dimensions: reception/production and oracy/literacy:

DIAGRAM 1: SPOKEN LANGUAGE SKILLS

Language (e.g. French)	Oracy	Literacy
Receptive skills	Listening	Reading
Productive skills	Speaking	Writing

There is a total of four distinct skills in learning a spoken language like French but eight such skills for a bilingual individual learning French and English. A similar table illustrates the skills involved in learning a sign language:

DIAGRAM 2: SIGN LANGUAGE SKILLS

Language (e.g. ISL)	Primary skills	Secondary skills
Receptive skills	Reading sign	Reading sign text
Productive skills	Signing	Sign writing

Efforts continue to create an orthography for signed languages but to date none have gained widespread acceptance (see for example, Sutton 2004). Some bilingual individuals may develop certain skills very well while other skills remain less well developed. We can use tables like these to assess a person's bilingual ability in more detail. Each skill can be divided into further sub-skills. Reading in a spoken language can vary from the simple to the complex. Signing can vary from that of the street to that of the lecture hall.

For Deaf people bilingualism may be mostly a question of four skills in two languages (reading sign, signing, reading, writing) and a range of abilities in two further skills (speaking, listening). For hearing people it is mainly a question of six skills: although there has been some development in creating systems of sign writing these are not widely used. To add to this complexity, some linguists refer to a fifth language ability called inner thinking i.e. thinking in the language but not using any of the above abilities (see for example, Skutnabb-Kangas 1981).

Cognitive academic language proficiency (CALP) is a term used to describe the language world of education and schooling. This concept is contrasted with conversational fluency or surface fluency, which is sometimes referred to as basic interpersonal communicative skills (BICS) (Cummins 2000). Academic competence (CALP) in a second language may take 5–8 years to develop while conversational fluency (BICS) takes 2 or 3 years of learning. If these concepts have validity we might want to think about their significance for sign languages because of their exclusion from the educational arena in the past. Are there difficulties in establishing a cognitive/academic language proficiency (CALP) in a language like sign language, which has been excluded from use in education? Moreover, if there are difficulties are these easily overcome?

A bilingual's use of two languages is also called functional bilingualism and here the focus is on the language usage by individuals with different targets (people) and in various language contexts (domains). Baker (2002) has drawn up a list of targets and contexts in which individuals can plot their use of different languages:

DIAGRAM 3: TARGETS AND CONTEXTS IN LANGUAGE LEARNING

Targets	**Contexts**
Nuclear family	Shopping
Extended family	Visual/auditory media
Work colleagues	Print media
Friends	Cinema
Neighbours	Work
Religious leaders	Correspondence/telephone
Teachers	Clubs/societies/organisations/sport

We could design scales that would help us plot the use of two languages by Deaf individuals with various persons and in different domains. For example, Deaf individuals could track their language use with the following people:

DIAGRAM 4: PEOPLE AND DOMAINS IN LANGUAGE LEARNING

	Always ISL	More ISL than English	Equal use of ISL and English	More English than ISL	Always English
Father					
Mother					
Brothers/sisters					
Friends/class					
Friends/home					
Teachers					
Friends/playground					
Neighbours					

Then the focus can be changed to the particular language that those people use with the Deaf person. A similar chart to plot the use of English/ISL by a Deaf person in various contexts e.g. shopping, the media, etc can be drawn up. There are some limitations with this kind of measurement of bilingual usage. Firstly, it is difficult to cover all the various targets and domains that could possibly exist. Secondly, the amount of time and frequency of exposure is not shown in either the contexts or targets. Lastly, because these measures are self-rating, people may exaggerate or give a 'halo' version of their language usage.

Bilingualism and cognition: is bilingualism good for the brain?

Research into the relationship between bilingualism and intelligence as measured by an IQ score, can be divided into three phases. In the first phase, research indicated that bilingualism had a detrimental effect on cognitive functioning. Saer (1923) claimed that monolinguals had a ten-point advantage over bilinguals in their IQ scores. The second phase studies indicated that there were no differences between monolinguals and bilinguals. Jones (1959) concluded that bilingualism had a neutral effect in terms of its impact on IQ scores. Peal and Lambert (1962) compared 10-year old middle class Canadian bilinguals (French and English) with monolinguals. The bilinguals had well developed skills in both languages or were balanced bilinguals. The results of this study marked a third phase in the bilingual and monolingual debate: it found that bilingualism had cognitive advantages over monolingualism. Some of the benefits of bilingualism included greater mental flexibility, an increase in the capacity to think abstractly and independently of words, and better concept formation. While this study showed that bilingualism could have positive benefits, some questions remain to be answered. The sample of 110 children in the group was small so care has to be taken with generalisations from research based on such a small sample. The group chosen were all balanced bilinguals and they may all have had high IQ scores to start with so we have a chicken and egg situation. Is the bilingualism the cause of the high IQ or is the high IQ 'producing' well developed bilinguals?

The question of defining and measuring intelligence in terms of IQ scores and single correct answers has created some debate. That there may be a variety of correct answers to a single problem has given rise to a style of thinking called divergent (Hudson 1968) or creative thinking (Torrance 1974). This is in contrast to the convergent thinking style measured by an IQ test. So does bilingualism have a positive impact on divergent thinking? Some theorists hold that having two words for an object, concept or action, improves divergent thinking. There is some research evidence from Cummins (1977) suggesting that if a bilingual achieves a threshold level or a well developed second language (balanced bilingualism) then positive benefits occur in divergent thinking.

The ability to think and reflect on the nature and functions of a language has been referred to as metalinguistic awareness. Early observation of bilinguals and monolinguals suggest that bilinguals focused on the meaning of words while monolinguals paid more attention to the sound of words (Ianco-Worrall 1972). Bialystok (1987) found that bilinguals (5–9 year olds) made superior syntactic or grammatical judgements than did monolingual children. Thus, bilinguals seem to have advantages over monolinguals with better analysis and processing of language internally. This in turn may facilitate an early reading readiness and acquisition of reading skills. However, we do not know if the advantages of increased metalinguistic awareness are permanent or temporary.

Bilingualism, cognition and Deaf people

The relationship between deafness and cognition has been of interest to researchers for some time. As for the debate concerning bilingualism and intelligence, three phases of thinking can be identified in relation to deafness and cognition. Early research on deaf children appeared to indicate that Deaf people were cognitively inferior to hearing people (Pintner, Eisenson and Staunton 1941). At a later stage this was revised and Myklebust (1953) claimed that in quantitative terms Deaf and hearing people were similar but that in qualitative terms the thinking of Deaf people was inferior. This led to the concept that Deaf people's intelligence was more concrete than that of hearing people and that Deaf people were less capable of abstract thinking. Later in the 1960s when linguistic factors were taken into account, performance tests showed that the range of intellectual abilities among Deaf people was similar to that found in the hearing population (Vernon 1967).

Into this picture came the recognition of sign language and the fact that it was a natural language. Arguments soon developed for the recognition of Deaf people as members of a bilingual community and for the provision of bilingualism in Deaf education. Can deaf children become balanced bilinguals and benefit from the cognitive advantages that may follow? This goal may be more easily attainable for deaf children with Deaf parents than for deaf children with hearing parents. If the child does not have adequate access to a signing environment then a sign language may not be adequately acquired as a first language. The level of bilingualism may not be good enough to benefit from the cognitive advantages that are supposed to come from bilingualism. Families with deaf children who opt for the bilingual route need the help of a good support structure.

Generally, when we refer to bilingualism and deafness we mean the combination of a sign language with a spoken language. This implies bimodal bilingualism, a combination not involved in spoken language bilingualism. Is modality important in terms of cognition and how does the brain cope with bimodal bilingualism? Hamers and Blanc (2000) reported on research into lateralization, i.e. certain functions are controlled by particular parts of the brain. Injury to the left hemisphere of the brain affects the sign language skills of fluent signers. Similarly, injury to the left hemisphere of the brain in hearing people affects their speech skills. Signers with right hemisphere injury can sign perfectly well even though signing is spatial and spatial skills are controlled by the right hemisphere of the brain. However, processing of non-verbal spatial skills is affected in these signers (Bellugi, Poizner and Klima 1993). All intact bilingual signers, whether they are Deaf or hearing, appear to show left hemisphere specialization for language (Corina, Vaid and Bellugi 1992). The evidence suggests that languages in general, irrespective of their modality, are processed in the left side of the brain. While the modality difference between sign and spoken language may appear on the surface to be significant, this difference may not be of great importance for the brain.

Bilinguals in society: a rare or a common phenomenon?

We now move away from themes related to the individual and look at bilingualism in a community, group or region. Some groups, who are bilingual, may live together in a region, e.g. Basques in Spain. Others, like Chinese people in the U.S or Deaf people in hearing society, may live scattered across communities and regions. Do we tend to think about Deaf people in terms of individuals who are bilingual or as a group who are bilingual in society or as both? There is evidence to suggest that bilingualism is a widespread phenomenon in the world. We find bilinguals among all major categories of populations, including different age groups and social classes and in nearly every country of the world (Crystal 1987). Bilinguals are not unusual and when bilinguals are combined with multilinguals they may form between 50% and 66% of the world's population. There is also the added feature that some forms of bilingualism may be on the increase with growing trade, travel and communications making language contact more frequent (Baker 2002).

The location of a language is often related to a geographical area, e.g. a region or country or homeland. Deaf people do not have a homeland. Immigrants may be separated from their homeland but they may have a chance of returning at some stage. Deaf people do not have a homeland to turn towards. Consequently, Deaf people live among hearing people. Many users of a language live in a community and this helps to maintain and transmit the language to children. The dispersal of Deaf populations has a weakening affect on their languages. Such a weakening factor may be reduced by the tendency for Deaf people to live in urban centres and in locations where relevant services are better. This context also allows a community network to develop, based more around social, cultural and linguistic ties than on geographical location. There may also be some opportunities for Deaf people to use sign language at work, e.g. in institutions like a Centre for Deaf Studies. Over the past century and a half, special schools, while educating deaf children, also served as vehicles for transmitting sign language despite strong opposition from school authorities at certain times (McDonnell and Saunders 1993). More recently, the change from special schooling to various kinds of integrated settings may result in fewer opportunities for deaf children to socialise with their peers.

Language planning in society

Fishman (1972) described diglossia as a situation in which two languages exist side-by-side in society and argued that the boundaries that separate two such languages are not permanent. Instability arises out of language contact and minority languages tend to lose out to more powerful languages. In one justification for language planning and protection Garcia (1992) compares the languages of the world to a garden of flowers in what is called the 'Language Garden Analogy.' A garden with a variety of flowers is more interesting and richer than a garden with one or two kinds. In the same way, a world with a multiplicity of languages makes a more interesting tapestry. Thus, planning is preferable to a laissez-faire policy. In such planning, the teachers are the gardeners and the politicians and policy makers are the landscape engineers. In order for diversity in the language garden to be maintained, careful attention is needed as some flowers spread and others need nurturing.

Others argue that language diversity makes the language world more difficult to tend and a standard monochrome garden is less trouble and expense. Attitudes to language can vary along a continuum—from those who favour an evolutionary approach in which the strongest survive and the weakest die, to preservationist attitudes that focus on preserving the status quo and blocking change. Between these extremes is the conservationist view, which argues for variety and that minority languages need the protection of language planning.

Language planning can be seen as 'deliberate efforts to influence the behaviour of others with respect to the acquisition, structure, or functional allocation of the language codes' (Cooper 1989:45). There are three important elements to language planning. Firstly, status planning is an attempt to maintain and increase the use of a language in as many domains or institutions as possible. Courts, governments, institutions (local and national), education and the media are some examples where a minority language may or may not be used. Initially, recognition of the language is sought to make its status official. Secondly, corpus planning refers to the fact that languages change and vocabularies must be modernized, e.g. in areas such as science and information technology. New terminology is created and standardised. The Catalans, Basques, Welsh and Irish use corpus planning to help coordinate change and development in this area. Thirdly, acquisition planning is concerned with the transmission of a language from one generation to another. This is important for minority languages, as some parents will always use a majority language with children because it might give the child a perceived advantage. So a language shift may take place. If a minority language is not transmitted to children in the family this task falls to the educational system.

Language planners aim to maintain the vitality of a spoken language through various measures to avoid language shift and decline. In general it could be argued that minority language monolingualism is impractical in today's world; minority languages require bilingualism or multilingualism. Additive bilingualism maintains the use of minority languages but subtractive bilingualism allows the majority language to undermine the minority language and replace it (Lambert 1974).

Language planning and Deaf people

The nature of the language planning measures taken in regard to Deaf people depends on the particular perspective on deafness that is predominant at a particular time. The main focus of planning in the past was to make Deaf education monolingual and to develop the dominant spoken language i.e. English in Ireland among the Deaf population. This kind of assimilationist planning occurred at various levels from official government reports (The Education of Children Who are Handicapped by Impaired Hearing 1972), to conference proposals (Lane 1984:394–5), to decisions made by parents on the advice of various experts (Crean 1997:47). We can see this as a form of status planning since the aim is to extend and maintain the use of English at the expense of sign language. The policies of oralism and total communication were basically monolingual in aspiration. Considerable effort also went into acquisition planning to try to ensure that deaf children developed skills in the dominant spoken language.

Another interesting area is the development of total communication and the mapping of signs on the English language. The various manually coded English systems were devised by borrowing signs from native sign languages, such as BSL and ISL, and inventing signs to suit the grammar of English, e.g. specific signs to refer to -ed (past), -s (plural), -ing (verb participle). These policies and plans not only posed linguistic difficulties; in terms of language planning they took only the norms of the hearing society into account. The linguistic needs, norms and values of Deaf people were largely ignored. Fasold (1984:257) claims that 'language is such a personal affair that real change is only possible with the consent of the user.' The sort of change that planners envisaged in Deaf education failed to involve Deaf people and did not recognise that sign language had its own grammar separate from English.

From a linguistic viewpoint, the life of a Deaf person is a complex one and assimilation policies have not recognised this reality. It could be argued that Deaf people move in and out of two languages and two cultures. At one level, sign language is often the language used by Deaf adults in their homes and social lives. There is also the increasing use of sign language in new areas (domains) because of the presence of interpreter services and a greater public acceptance of sign language in society (e.g. in education, T.V., medicine, law). At another level, Deaf people live in a world heavily influenced by the dominant language, i.e. English here in Ireland. The childhood homes and places of work or education for the majority of Deaf people are English speaking. In these contexts, signers may use a form of signing that is heavily influenced by English. The use of text telephoning, T.V. subtitles and speed text operators in further education makes English more accessible to Deaf people.

There is also the question of storing and transmitting information in the Deaf community. While some of this is done through signed video, written English is still very important. Will future planning bring forms of sign writing into widespread use and will computer technology facilitate the development of new ways of transmitting information? These remain open questions. However, we urgently need language planning initiatives that would assist acquisition of sign language in early childhood and the development of literacy skills during the school years.

Bilingualism in education

It is important to distinguish between two basic varieties of bilingual education (Baker 2002):

(i) transitional bilingual education (weak forms of bilingualism)
(ii) maintenance bilingual education (strong forms of bilingualism).

The aims and goals of both kinds of bilingual programmes are different. Transitional bilingual education aims at assimilation of minority groups and involves a move or shift from the minority language to the majority language. These bilingual programmes are of little interest to advocates of bilingualism in Deaf education. Those who support bilingualism in Deaf education favour a strong form of bilingualism. They want to see both languages promoted, with sign language as the first language and the dominant spoken language as the second language. Maintenance bilingual education aims to foster and maintain the minority language which generally involves the use of a minority language as the medium of instruction in school. The majority language is introduced as a second language subject or to teach 10%–50% of the curriculum (Baker 2002:209). Different terms are used when referring to this kind of programme with minority spoken languages—'developmental maintenance', 'heritage language', 'native', 'ethnic', 'minority', 'ancestral', and 'aboriginal.'

A strong bilingual programme that aims to foster the two languages has some important features. At least 50% of the school curriculum has to be taught through the minority language. One important aim includes saving the minority language and giving fluency in the second language. Parental support for such a programme is also a crucial factor for the success of this option. Major reviews of maintenance programmes relating to spoken languages were carried out by Cummins (1993) and Dutcher (1995) who concluded that minority children in developmental maintenance programmes suffered no loss in their performance on the various curricular subject areas.

On the question of performance in their second language (often English) it is surprising to find that minority students attending developmental maintenance programmes with 50% or less input in their second language had comparable results with other minority students who received all their instruction through their second language in mainstream education. One explanation for this is that the use of a minority language in education helps both the self-esteem and the first language skills of a learner. These benefits in turn are transferred to help in learning a second language. Consequently, we must consider the possibility that self-esteem and second language literacy among Deaf students would benefit from the use of ISL in a developmental maintenance programme. Dutcher (1995) in a paper prepared for the World Bank, looked at the economics and value for money of developmental maintenance bilingual education. She examined elementary bilingual education in several countries and concluded that development of a mother tongue was important for cognitive development and provided a platform for learning the second language. She also found that parental support and community involvement were important ingredients for a successful outcome. In addition, she claimed that strong forms of bilingualism are not any more expensive to run than other programmes; in fact they can have important cost savings because they are associated with faster progress and higher levels of achievement among students, as well as lower levels of unemployment and higher levels of skills in the workforce. Weak forms of bilingual education may be more costly in the long run because of slower progress, lower levels of achievement and the need for compensatory or special education among students; drop out rates may also be high, adding further cost to the economy because of reduced employment possibilities.

Bilingualism in the school and classroom

In a bilingual situation where majority and minority languages like English and Irish Sign Language are used, the boundaries between the languages are important and need to be established. The bilingual classroom may try to separate the two languages and have clear boundaries for their use, or it may aim at a more integrated or concurrent use of the two languages. We need to reflect on how Irish Sign Language would best be used with English in the bilingual classroom.

There are several arguments for having a separation of languages in the bilingual classroom. Firstly, for bilingualism to exist in a stable manner in society, people usually use one language for certain functions and situations, e.g. at home, and another language for work, education, and so on (Fishman 1972). Consequently, some researchers claim that languages need to be separated in the classroom to mirror this division of language use in society. Secondly, many bilingual homes follow the principle of one parent one language. Bilingualism in Deaf education may work well in team teaching situations where one teacher uses Irish Sign Language and the other English.

Schools may also try to establish a clear boundary between the languages by teaching some subjects through one language and allocating other subjects to a second language. In Deaf education one way of establishing a boundary between the languages would be to use sign language for discursive activities while reading and writing in English could be used to reinforce this work.

Conclusion

In this article I have attempted to examine how bilingualism impacts in a positive way both on the individual and on society. I have also attempted to highlight some of the salient features of bilingualism in education and school. Due consideration was also given to how these ideas might apply to the Deaf population.

The essential elements in the relationship between bilingualism and deafness contain nothing dramatically new. I have already mentioned how sign language and literacy have always been part of the literature on deafness. However, recent linguistic studies of sign languages and the application of bilingual theory and practice to Deaf studies have projected a new framework onto existing ideas. This merger of linguistics and Deaf studies is best illustrated in general texts on bilingualism. Hamers and Blanc (2000) and Baker (2002) both refer to Deaf bilinguals and bring Deaf studies into mainstream linguistic inquiry. Ireland has started to recognise not only that Deaf people use two languages in their daily lives but also that the Deaf community (using ISL and English) may be relatively more successful than the majority of the hearing population (using Irish and English) in conducting their daily lives in two languages.

References

Baker, C. (2002) *Foundations of Bilingual Education and Bilingualism*, Clevedon: Multilingual Matters.

Bellugi, U., Poizner, H. and Klima, E.S. (1993) Language modality and the brain, in A.H. Johnson (ed) *Brain Development and Cognition: A Reader*. Oxford: Blackwell.

Bialystok, E. (1987) Words as things: development of work concepts by bilingual children, *Studies in Second Language Learning*, 9:133–140.

Bloomfield, L. (1933) *Language*, New York: Holt.

Cooper, R.L. (1989) *Language Planning and Social Change*, Cambridge: Cambridge University Press.

Corina, D.P., Vaid, J. and Bellugi, U. (1992) The linguistic basis of left hemisphere specialization, *Science*, 255:1258–60.

Crean, E. (1997) *Breaking the Silence: The Education of the Deaf in Ireland 1816–1996*, Dublin: Irish Deaf Society Publications.

Crystal, D. (1987) *The Cambridge Encyclopedia of Language*, Cambridge: Cambridge University Press.

Cummins, J. (1977) Cognitive factors associated with the attainment of intermediate levels of bilingual skills, *Modern Language Journal*, 61:3–12.

—— (1993) The research base for heritage language promotion, in M. Danesi, K. Mc Leod and S. Morris (eds.) *Heritage Languages and Education: The Canadian Experiment*, Oakville: Mosaic Press.

—— (1997) Cultural and linguistic diversity in education: a mainstream issue? *Educational Review* 49(2): 105–114

—— (2000) Putting language proficiency in its place: responding to critiques of the conversational/academic language distinction, in J. Cenoz and U. Jessner (eds) *English in Europe: The Acquisition of a Third Language*, Clevedon: Multilingual Matters.

Dutcher, N. (1995) *The Use of first and Second Languages in Education: A Review of International Experience*, Washington, D.C.: World Bank.

Fasold, R. (1984) *The Sociolinguistics of Society*, Oxford: Blackwell.

Fishman, J.A. (1972) *The Sociology of Language*, Rowley, MA: Newbury House.

Garcia, O. (1992) *Societal Bilingualism and Multilingualism (Mimeo)*, New York: City University of New York.

Hamers, J.F. and Blanc, M.H.A. (2nd ed.) (2000) *Bilinguality and Bilingualism*, Cambridge: Cambridge University Press.

Hudson, L. (1968) *Frames of Mind*, Harmondsworth, Middlesex: Penguin.

Ianco-Worrall, A.D. (1972) Bilingualism and cognitive development, *Child Development*, 43:1390–1400.

Jones, W.R. (1959) *Bilingualism and Intelligence*, Cardiff: University of Wales Press.

Lambert, W.E. (1974) Culture and Language as factors in learning and education, in F.E. Aboud and R.D. Meade (eds) *Cultural Factors in Learning and Education 5th Western Washington Symposium on Learning*, Bellingham, Washington.

Lane, H. (1984) *When the Mind Hears*, New York: Random House.

Lewis, E.G. (1981) *Bilingualism and Bilingual Education*, Oxford: Pergamon.

McDonnell, P. and Saunders, H. (1993) Sit on your hands: strategies to prevent signing, in R. Fisher and H. Lane (eds) *Looking back: A Reader on the History of Deaf Communities and their Sign Languages*, Hamburg: Signum Press.

Myklebust, H. (1953) Towards a new understanding of the Deaf child, *American Annals of the Deaf*, 98:345–357.

Peal, E. and Lambert, W.E. (1962) The relationship of bilingualism to intelligence, *Psychological Monographs*, 76(27): 1–23.

Pintner, R., Eisenson, J. and Stanton, M. (1941) *The Psychology of the Physically Handicapped*, New York: Croft.

Saer, D. J. (1923) The effects of bilingualism on intelligence, *British Journal of Psychology*, 14:25–38.

Skutnabb-Kangas, T. (1981) *Bilingualism or Not: The Education of Minorities*, Clevedon: Multilingual Matters.

Stokoe, W. (1960) *Sign language structure: An outline of the visual communication systems of the American Deaf, Occasional Papers No.8*, University of Buffalo.

Sutton, V. (2004) The Deaf Action Committee for Sign Writing, *Website*: http://www.signwriting.org (March 6).

Swedish National Association for the Deaf (1991) *Action Programme on Sign Language*, Stockholm.

The Education of Children Who are Handicapped by Impaired Hearing (1972), Report of a Committee appointed by the Minister of Education, Dublin: Stationary Office.

Torrance, E.P. (1974) *Torrance Tests of Creative Thinking: Directions Manual and Scoring Guide*, Lexington, MA: Ginn.

Vernon, M. (1967) Relationship of language to the thinking process, *Archives of General Psychiatry*, 16:325–333.

Woll, B. (1990) Sign Language, in N.E Collinge (ed.) *An Encyclopedia of Language*, London: Routledge.

Ireland and Finland: A comparative study of two Deaf communities

John Bosco Conama

Introduction

This chapter presents a comparative case study of the Deaf communities in Ireland and Finland. There are a lot of potential benefits to be gained in undertaking comparative cross-national studies. Cross-national comparative studies of Deaf issues are not commonplace but examples of this kind of analysis have begun to appear recently. For instance, the World Federation of the Deaf published an international survey on the national education system for deaf children in several countries in 1991 (Skutnabb-Kangas and Phillipson 1994). An investigation of the status of sign language in seventeen countries carried out by the European Union of the Deaf is another example (Kyle and Allsop 1997).

Barcham (1998) points out that due to the continued exchange of information at a superficial level, it is possible to work in the field of special education in one country with no reference to what happens elsewhere. She believes more in-depth international comparisons would enhance the understanding of the development of policies and practices in Deaf education in one's own country (*ibid* 246). May (1998, 21) points out that economic globalisation may internationalise welfare production and that there may be a long-term process of convergence underway. This would strengthen the role of comparative analysis.

Even considering the difficulties involved, a comparative study is still an attractive option since it offers an international dimension that certainly enhances our understanding of where the Irish situation stands in relation to other countries. May (*ibid* 185) describes four different approaches to comparative research: an 'import-mirror' view, a 'difference' view, a 'theory-development' view and a 'prediction' view. These approaches are not distinct as a comparative exercise might apply more than one approach.

The first approach, import-mirror, refers to those studies in which comparisons are made between one country and another in order to interpret policies and practices more clearly. This view might be useful for those who want to introduce practices from abroad into their own country. The second approach, difference, refers to studies which set out to explain the cultural, social, political or economic differences between countries. This approach is crucial to understanding similarities and diversities of policies between countries. It is related to a third approach, theory-development, in which academics have developed the 'difference' model by using the comparisons to generate theoretical generalisations and explanations. Most prominent among these is the typology of welfare regimes developed by Esping-Andersen (1990). Finally, the prediction approach refers to the potential outcomes of particular policies after examining cultural, social, political and economic contexts in many countries. The Organisation for Economic Co-operation and Development (OECD) is a prime example of an organisation doing this type of work (May 1998:185–89).

For the purposes of this study, the first view described by May is the most appropriate although it is not suggested that we should introduce practices into Ireland similar to those in Finland. In the next section, I explain the methodology used in the study. I then explain the choice of Finland for comparative analysis in terms of its historical, social and political background. This is followed by a brief description of the Finnish Deaf community and its history, which provides a necessary context within which the socio-economic status of Finnish Deaf people can be compared with that of their Irish counterparts. A number of brief comparative references to important social services are also made. To conclude, the lessons arising from the comparison are noted.

Methodology

The methodology of this comparative study is simple. Barcham's case study of the Finnish Deaf community and the author's personal correspondence with officials of the Finnish Association of the Deaf provides the nucleus of the information contained in this chapter.[1] A number of documents and reports provided by the Finnish Association of the Deaf constitute further sources of information. Publications from international organisations such as the OECD are also utilised. As for the Irish part, information collated for a master's thesis (Conama 2002), provided a starting point. This information was obtained from official reports, academic articles and social policy publications. The representative organisation of the Irish Deaf community, the Irish Deaf Society, provided information as well through its research reports and quarterly journals.

Finland and Ireland

Finland was intentionally chosen because of its many similarities to Ireland. Both countries are geographically situated on the periphery of Europe, which affects their ability to influence mainland European politics. Both countries are members of the European Union and are militarily neutral, and both have relatively small populations. Finland with 5 million people has a slightly larger population than Ireland with just fewer than 4 million (OECD 1999). While Finnish society has linguistic diversity, with a number of minority languages especially in the border areas, bilingualism—English and Irish—is dominant in Ireland. Both once had a dominant agricultural economy but now depend heavily on manufactured exports to sustain their economies (Singleton 1998).

TABLE 1: BASIC DATA, IRELAND AND FINLAND (2003)

	Ireland	*Finland*
Population	3,917,336 (2002)	5,112,000 (1995)
Area size (square miles)	27,137	130,524
Official language(s)	Irish	Finnish
	English	Swedish
		Sami
		Sign Language (FinSL)
GNP per capita in US$	$30,002	$26,502
Growth of GDP (1998)	8.9%	3.5%
Unemployment rate (2003)	4.6%	8.9%

(Sources: OECD 2003; Eurostat 2003; Ireland 2002)

Their economies are small and open and have no significant influence on the world economy. They are susceptible to the effects of the global economic shifts (OECD 1999). Both countries have experienced high unemployment rates when in economic recession. However, Finland's high rate of unemployment is a recent phenomenon (*ibid*) while the Irish experienced a long period of high unemployment before the 'Celtic Tiger' economy emerged.

Both countries have a colonial past and a significant neighbouring world power (i.e. Russia and Sweden with Finland, Britain with Ireland). One major difference between their colonial experiences was that Finland had localised government, which gave the Finnish population a degree of cultural and social autonomy and which did not lead to any sustained effort at mass assimilation. Ireland, in contrast, experienced centralised power from London and also experienced attempts at religious and linguistic assimilation. Interestingly, in the 19th century, both countries experienced catastrophic famines that resulted in the deaths of thousands of people, though far more casualties were recorded in Ireland. The Irish perspective on this disaster tends to be more politicised than the Finnish view of their famine. The Finns regard theirs as an ecological disaster rather than a case of economic mismanagement as happened in the Irish case (NESC 1992; Singleton 1998).

Welfare regimes

Although there are similarities between both countries, there are significant cultural and social differences. These differences are reflected particularly in social policy responses to the needs of their populations. To understand these differences, it is useful to draw on comparative research—with particular reference to the third approach described above, theory development—which attempts to classify national welfare systems and social policies. Esping-Andersen's work (1990) has provided the most prominent analytical model in this area. Esping-Andersen developed a typology of three welfare regimes. He measured the social policy responses of each country on the basis of decommodification and social stratification. Decommodification refers to how independent an individual can be without depending on labour market income and social stratification refers to the extent to which social policy responses ameliorate social class structures (*ibid* 35–79).

The first regime—known as the social democratic welfare regime—is rated high in terms of decommodification and is regarded as a strong exponent of socialism in terms of ameliorating social stratification. These are characteristic features of welfare provision in the Scandinavian countries. In contrast, conservative / corporatist welfare regimes are typical in central European countries such as Germany and Austria. In this type of regime, decommodification is measured as average while conservatism remains strong in terms of social stratification. The third type of regime is known as a liberal welfare regime. This regime is ranked low in terms of decommodification and is a strong exponent of liberalism. Countries such as the USA, Britain and Canada fall into this category. Broadly speaking, the typology would place these regimes as follows in descending order of their degree of egalitarianism: social democratic, corporatist and liberal. Although Esping-Andersen places Ireland in the liberal and Finland in the conservative category, he recognises that a number of social policy measures in Finland makes it more like the social democratic model.

However, Esping-Andersen's work is not universally accepted, and other theorists have identified shortcomings in his typology of welfare regimes. In a feminist critique, Lewis (1994) pointed out that women's unpaid work was not recognised in the typology. Other researchers argue that there are more than three types of welfare regimes. Leibfried (1993) identified a Latin Rim model and Castles and Mitchell (1993) proposed four clusters of welfare regimes. Ireland's location in these classifications, however, is problematic due to its unique history and social development (O'Donnell 1999:70–90). Most social researchers agree that a typology of welfare regimes makes a considerable contribution to understanding cross-national differences (*ibid*). It is now generally agreed that Finland belongs to the social democratic cluster while Ireland fits into the liberal model (Hill 1996:38–58). Therefore, it is clear that Finland and Ireland have different welfare regimes.

Finland recognises social benefits as a right of citizens and administers universal social services, which citizens can avail of regardless of their income or status (Sainbury 1994). Despite experiencing a deep economic recession in the 1990s and a subsequent recovery, the Finnish government has vowed to adhere to what they describe as 'the Nordic welfare society' (OECD 1999). As the Finns develop their rights-based welfare regime, their country has been recognised as one of most progressive, tolerant and wealthy countries in the world (Singleton 1998).

By contrast, the Irish welfare philosophy has been historically dominated by the principle that welfare benefits are residual and based on need. Before Ireland experienced its 'Celtic Tiger' economic boom, it was seen as a conservative European backwater (O'Donnell 1999: 70–90). Anti-intellectualism, clerical control and continued economic protectionism of the economy coloured the international perception of Ireland (Chubb 1992:19–20).

In summary then, Ireland and Finland have very significant structural similarities and certain historical experiences in common. However, they possess very different welfare regimes, reflecting differences in political ideology. In the next section, we attempt to see if these regime differences are reflected in policies and outcomes with regard to the respective Deaf communities.

The Finnish Deaf community

The Finnish Deaf community has been publicly prominent in the global discussion of Deaf issues. Internationally, it is often regarded as being one of the most progressive and advanced Deaf communities. This perception is reflected in the re-election of a Finnish Deaf woman, Liisa Kauppinen, as the president of the World Federation of the Deaf (WFD) in July 1999 and the election of her successor, Markku Jokinen in 2003, a Finnish Deaf man. The office of WFD is currently situated in Finland. The Finnish Deaf community has been able to provide a number of experts to the WFD to sit on special commissions on a number of critical issues. It has been prominent in aiding Deaf communities in the developing world. The Finnish Deaf Association has sponsored community projects to empower Deaf communities in Tanzania and Uganda. Along with the Finnish Ministry of Foreign Affairs it has also sponsored regional conferences on Deaf-related issues and has enabled local Deaf delegates to attend (FAD, 2003).

Statistically, there is no actual census of Deaf people in Finland. However, according to the Finnish Association of the Deaf, there are about 5,000 Deaf people, reflecting a rule of thumb ratio of 1:1,000 Deaf people in the general population (FAD 1999a). Most Deaf people are concentrated in southern Finland since the social and economic infrastructure there enables them to obtain a relatively higher standard of living. However, they are not concentrated in specific areas but are geographically scattered throughout the southern cities (*ibid*).

The association also estimates that 80 per cent of Finnish Deaf people possess fluency in FinSL (Finnish Sign Language) and, overall, that approximately 14,000 people among the national population possess an 'average understanding' of FinSL. In 1995, Finnish Sign Language, along with other minority languages such as Sami and Swedish, were recognised by the state constitution. This has had significant implications for the citizenship rights of Finnish Deaf people (FAD 1998). A national centre for sign language research has been established. The state has also set up a commission known as the Finnish Sign Language Board to implement and monitor measures aiming to promote and support FinSL (FAD 1999a). Both initiatives can be seen as a state response to constitutional recognition of FinSL. To understand the current situation of the Finnish Deaf community, one has to look at the historical background to explain how they managed to achieve what they have achieved. We can then compare their history with the Irish experience.

Though the state has now acknowledged FinSL, like many countries Finland has had a long history of sign language oppression. Finland implemented the oralist philosophy of Deaf education in the late 1890s and abolished their former system, which was based on the French method and which used what was known as 'methodical signing' (Lane 1984:58–64). The experience is broadly similar to what occurred in Ireland although the context is somewhat different. 'Methodical signing' survived in the Irish Catholic schools until the 1940s but was eradicated in the Protestant-run schools in the 1890s (Crean 1996).

Formal education for the Deaf came earlier to Irish children than to their Finnish counterparts. The first known Irish school was opened in 1816 (Matthews 1996) while a Finnish Deaf man, after returning from Sweden, opened the first school in Porvoo in 1846 (FAD 1999a). There is no record of how Finnish deaf children were educated prior to the establishment of this school. From that point on, both countries saw the opening of a number of Deaf schools to cater for the educational needs of deaf children.

Like many countries in Europe, Deaf education in Finland experienced the fallout from the 1880 Milan conference (FAD 1999a). The momentum to embrace the oralist philosophy that believed in banishing sign language from schools and substituting speech training began in the Scandinavian countries during the 1870s. It came to prominence in Finland towards the end of the nineteenth century where there was resistance against it and Deaf people decided to form a representative organisation in 1905—The Finnish Association of the Deaf—to protect and uphold the status of FinSL (Barcham 1998:249).

In Ireland, however, there is no recorded resistance against the implementation of oralism, especially in the 1890s and later in the 1940s. There is some speculation that in the 1880s Francis Maginn, the founder of the British Deaf Association, attempted to establish a similar organisation for Ireland but received little support from Irish Deaf people. As for the 1940s and 1950s, there is no clear explanation for the lack of resistance among Irish Deaf people to the oralist approach. It is possible that severe economic stagnation, clerical control of educational and social institutions and the prevailing anti-intellectualism mentioned by Chubb (1992) were factors.

Oralism in Finland dominated the educational scene up to the mid-1970s and according to FAD it left a damaging legacy while failing to achieve its main objective—the eradication of FinSL (FAD 1999a). This legacy can be clearly seen in older generations of Deaf people who tend to be less confident in using FinSL in the public arena and fail to recognise FinSL as their own language (*ibid*). A number of harsh measures were employed to banish FinSL and older Deaf people remember being severely punished for using FinSL. Finland also experienced a eugenics campaign to reduce the number of Deaf people (Hietala 1996). In the 1930s, for example, Finnish law did not allow Deaf people to marry without getting permission from the President of Finland, a law that was not repealed until 1969.

The Irish Deaf experience can be seen as generally similar but more thoroughly documented especially since the 1940s. Oralism dominated the world of education for the Deaf for a very long period (Lane 1993) but it became dominant in the education provision for the Deaf in Ireland from the late 1950s. As for marriage, there was no specific legislation preventing Irish Deaf people from intermarrying.

The Finnish government set up a commission inquiring into the state of the education for the Deaf in 1973 (Barcham 1998). The commission concluded with a report stating that sign language had a part to play in the education of the Deaf but regarded it as an auxiliary and arbitrary language (*ibid* 250). This has a striking similarity to views expressed in a report on the education of Irish deaf children although the report did not reach any firm conclusion about the status of Irish Sign Language (ISL) (Department of Education 1972).

During the early 1980s, Finnish Deaf leaders decided to do something to protect the status of FinSL, which had been under constant attack, especially on the educational front. In this process, they developed a largely successful strategy to protect and promote the use of the FinSL (FAD 1999a). In 1987, a government curriculum document was published which placed an emphasis on the education of deaf children within this context. It recognised bilingualism as the appropriate approach for educating deaf children and stated that any attempt to use FinSL and spoken Finnish simultaneously would result in a 'pidgin' language. In 1990, the government curriculum document went further and recognised FinSL as the first language of deaf children (Barcham 1998:250).

To have the government acknowledging the status of FinSL in the late 1980s was a pioneering development in itself and ahead of other countries including Ireland. During the 1980s in Ireland there was no official investigation as to the status of Irish Sign Language nor was any serious attempt made to establish an official investigation. The Finnish strategy was rewarded in the following decade with the incorporation of FinSL as a minority language in the state constitution in 1995 (FAD 1999a). A dedicated research centre and a state sponsored FinSL Board have since been established (*ibid*).

In contrast, developments in Ireland happened much more slowly. A representative organisation—the Irish Deaf Society (IDS)—was formed in 1981 after much dissatisfaction with the services being provided by existing organisations. The IDS was also established to mark the UN sponsored international year of disabled people (Irish Deaf Journal 1988). Since the establishment of the IDS, there had been no obvious long term strategy in place and a piecemeal approach was adopted in a campaign for state recognition of ISL. Judging by the lack of progress on this front, it is clear that this approach had not been successful. The piecemeal approach can be exemplified by one-off projects such as the survey of the Irish Deaf community in 1992 (Matthews 1996), individual studies such as research into the grammar of ISL (McDonnell 1996), European Union HORIZON initiatives to train ISL/English interpreters and ISL tutors, and a MAPS project to train Deaf adult trainers (MAPS 1999). These initiatives were not continued due to lack of funds and official indifference. However, since 2002 the Irish Deaf Society has adopted a more pro-active strategy of contacting politicians, political parties and government departmental officials directly and arguing its case. This has proved to be a successful approach and a number of research, advocacy and literacy projects have been approved and funded by the government (Irish Deaf Journal 2003).

Historically, both countries experienced the negative consequences of oralism and both Deaf communities have attempted to deal with its effects. There are similarities in historical processes between the Finnish and Irish Deaf communities. However, since the 1980s the Irish are still struggling with the consequences of history while the Finns have developed a set of policies to protect the status of FinSL. It is important at this point to examine specific policies towards the Deaf and the socio-economic status of Deaf people in both countries.

Socio-economic status of Deaf people

In this section, brief comparisons are made in relation to employment, education, literacy, social services and participation in policy.

Employment

Before the economic situation worsened in the 1990s, Finland enjoyed an average national unemployment rate of 5 per cent. Unemployment in the Deaf community was just under eight per cent (FAD 1999a). Thus, in Finland a Deaf person was roughly one and a half times more likely to be unemployed than his/her hearing counterpart. In Ireland during the same time period a Deaf person was three times more likely to be unemployed than his/her hearing compatriot (Swan 1994). However, in the transition from an industrial to an information age and with the collapse of its main trading partner, the Soviet Union, the unemployment rate in Finland worsened rapidly from the late 1980's onwards. The peak occurred in the mid-1990s when the general rate reached 15 per cent (OECD 1999). For the Deaf community, the rate climbed steeply, doubling to a rate of 30 per cent (FAD 1999a). This meant that Finnish Deaf people found themselves twice as likely to be unemployed as hearing people.

There has been a remarkable recovery in the Finnish economy since the mid-1990s, which has seen a gradual reduction in the general unemployment rate. In order to maximise the benefit of this recovery, the Finnish Association of the Deaf launched an employment project in 1997, which trained 12 Deaf career guidance counsellors and which was financed by the European Social Fund. The counsellors are expected to be employed in state employment centres to disseminate information and to advise Deaf clients on employment matters (FAD 1999b). The project aimed to maintain the independence of Deaf persons and increase the flexibility of employment options for them. This project is the first of its kind in Europe and is underpinned by the important principle of empowering Deaf people directly. The unemployment rate for the Finnish Deaf community should be reduced over the long term.

Education

There are 17 schools for the Deaf in Finland, all of which adopt a bilingual approach in the education of deaf children. The early acceptance of bilingualism in the Nordic countries made a huge impression on the Finnish education system for the Deaf (FAD 1997). However, only two Deaf schools employ Deaf teachers and there are very few hearing teachers who regard FinSL as their mother tongue, much to the dissatisfaction of the Finnish Deaf community. This has significant implications in that the quality of education delivery varies from school to school. The ongoing debate in Finland centres on teacher competency and their unfamiliarity with the recent establishment of bilingualism (FAD 1997; Barcham 1998).

However, the introduction of bilingualism was made easy by the social democratic attitude of the Finnish State department of education. FinSL was acknowledged as a teaching language in the early 1970s and was further advanced by becoming a school subject during the 1980s. The gradual acceptance of FinSL as an indigenous language was somewhat delayed by a debate centred on the alleged superiority of

Signed Finnish over FinSL. Nevertheless, linguistic and social research revealed the status of FinSL as a primary language. The acceptance of FinSL is reflected in the legislation approved by the Finnish parliament and its incorporation into the Finnish State constitution (FAD 1997; Barcham 1998).

The introduction of bilingualism is vindicated by the increase in the number of Deaf people entering third level education. It is generally estimated that one third of young Finnish Deaf people have entered third level education while among the older generation, the number was but a trickle (FAD 1999a). Although bilingualism has taken root in the Finnish system, this has not been the case in the Irish situation despite several efforts to have it established (MSDP Handbook 1998). The impact of bilingualism in Finland is reflected in the decision to have FinSL accepted as a university subject. Several doctoral theses investigating the status of FinSL have been submitted to universities. The establishment of a dedicated research centre further supports the infrastructure of bilingualism where a ten year long lexicographical study of FinSL has recently been completed and further measures to investigate the language are planned. The cultural and linguistic transmission of FinSL to future generations of deaf children is secure since the government sponsors a national scheme of free instruction in FinSL to hearing parents of deaf children. It is estimated that 95 per cent of deaf children in Finland are born to hearing parents (FAD 1999a).

It is safe to state that such an infrastructure is virtually non-existent in Ireland. This lack of understanding is reflected in a clause inserted in the Education Act whereby the state is expected to provide education to deaf children through 'Irish sign language or other sign languages' (Ireland 1999). The Model School for the Deaf Project set up a pre-school provision for deaf children and its leading principles are firmly within the bilingual philosophy (Irish Deaf Journal 2003). Bilingualism has not been embraced by those who direct education in Ireland despite the efforts of the IDS and the Model School for the Deaf to host information seminars (*ibid*). Compared to the Finnish situation, it seems it will be a number of years before Ireland can match the Finnish infrastructure or have ISL established as a university subject.

Literacy

In 1988, a survey was carried out to ascertain the reading level of deaf children in Finland. Like an Irish survey of 1991 (James and O'Neill 1991), the Finnish survey found that the reading skills of an average 15-year-old Deaf child corresponded to that of an 8-year-old hearing child (Hakkarainen 1988). This study was conducted before any substantive implementation of bilingualism occurred and was carried out even where signed Finnish was regularly used (FAD 1994). However, subsequent surveys, carried out after the introduction of bilingual education, indicate remarkable improvements on the 1988 survey. The improvements are exemplified in the literacy standard of deaf children having moved towards the national average and in the rising numbers of Deaf students entering third level education (*ibid*). The authors of these surveys identified a number of reasons for these improvements, such as the early language acquisition of FinSL by deaf children at home and the re-designated status of spoken Finnish as a foreign language in Deaf schools (*ibid*).

Comparatively, the Irish experience is similar to that reported in the 1988 Finnish survey but there has been no subsequent investigation into literacy levels of Irish deaf children. Moreover, up to the year 2000 no urgent action was undertaken to alleviate the literacy problems identified in the James and O'Neill (1991) survey. Recognising the literacy crisis within the Deaf community, the Department of Education and Science agreed to fund a five-year project aiming to build up a tutorial infrastructure for those who need to develop and improve their literacy skills (Irish Deaf Journal 2000).

Social services

It is worth mentioning that Finnish social policy responses have made considerable improvements in the services available to Deaf people. There are, for example, two full-time interpreting training centres, which ensure a regular supply of qualified FinSL interpreters. In addition, there are 20 interpreter referral centres throughout Finland. There are 24 salaried interpreters with many more freelance interpreters filling in the gaps (FAD 1997). Currently, two ambitious initiatives are under way to establish long distance interpreting services operated by a video-conferencing facility (FAD 2000).

By contrast, in Ireland there is only one agency handling interpreting assignments. I know of no salaried interpreter, while a small pool of interpreters are available to do assignments on a freelance basis (Irish Sign Link 2000). Since two one-off training courses for interpreters were held in this country, the campaign to set up a permanent centre for this purpose was launched by the Irish Deaf Society in the early 1990s and was intensively lobbied for in the late 1990s. This campaign culminated in the announcement to fund a Centre for Deaf Studies in Trinity College, Dublin, in June 2000 (Irish Deaf Journal 2000). The numbers of interpreters and ISL tutors are expected to increase in the years ahead.

On Finnish television, five-minute long news bulletins are transmitted daily through the medium of FinSL. A weekly programme, focussing on the Deaf community in Finland, is transmitted on Saturdays. With government financial support, the Finnish Association of the Deaf produces, on average, fourteen videotapes a year, a copy of which is sent to Deaf people throughout the country. The videos contain bulletins of important news, current affairs and discussion about cultural and social life in Finland. The presentation is given entirely in FinSL. Recently, the national broadcaster appointed a Deaf editor to manage the daily 'News in Sign Language' programmes (FAD 1997).

In comparison, Ireland has a daily two-minute long news bulletin transmitted on television through ISL. In addition, it has a total of six hours a year devoted to the TV programme 'Hands On' which addresses Deaf community issues. There is no comparable video scheme or Deaf editor in this country. A survey on socio-economic conditions faced by Deaf people suggests that the recent economic successes in Ireland have not been passed on to benefit the Deaf community (Conama and Grehan 2002; Poverty Today 2002).

Policy participation

The Deaf community in Finland have participated at state level in terms of formulating language and communication policies towards the Deaf community. This participation is guided by two principles: that FinSL is the language of the Deaf community and that the Deaf community is regarded as a cultural and linguistic minority. Official recognition of

 FinSL and the establishment of the Finnish Sign Language Board are clear results of this policy-making participation. The Board contains a number of Deaf persons working with civil servants to identify and implement the necessary measures to promote and uphold the status of FinSL in Finnish society (FAD 1999a). This is only one example of representatives of the Deaf community and the state working together. There are others. In 1997, for example, a special working group, which included a number of Deaf representatives, investigated the rights of those who use sign language, and published a report. The group was established under the aegis of the Finnish Ministry of Justice, exemplifying the extent of participation in the consultative process by Deaf people. The report identified the main obstacles to those who want to use FinSL comprehensively and offered a number of proposals to eliminate these obstacles (Finnish Working Group 1997).

There is a stark difference between the two countries in the extent to which control over projects is entrusted to Deaf people. Control of the employment project to train Deaf career guidance counsellors, and funded by the European Social Fund, for example, was entrusted to the Finnish Association of the Deaf (FAD 1999a). This reflects the confidence and belief of the Finnish state and the EU in the ability of FAD to administer such a project on behalf of its sponsors. In Ireland, a similar application by the Irish Deaf Society was rejected in favour of an application by a consortium of paternalistic service providers, which subsequently employed two hearing career guidance counsellors to cater specifically for Deaf job seekers (Irish Deaf Society 2000).

The examples of the empowerment of Deaf people in real terms are striking, especially since Finland has only recently recovered from the deep economic recession of the early 1990s. It illustrates that the civil rights of Deaf people are both respected and recognised and that their needs continue to be met by different services regardless of Finland's priorities for economic restructuring and recovery. The Irish experience is different and two case studies of two specific policy issues—education for the Deaf and access to broadcasting (Conama 2002; Conama and Grehan 2002) have demonstrated the serious marginalisation of Irish Deaf people. The research found that consultation with Deaf people was of a minimal and superficial nature and therefore they had no real input into policy-making. Given the importance of these issues to the

Deaf community, it is fair to expect that empowerment of Deaf people to participate in policy-making processes is almost non-existent.

Conclusions

It has to be stressed that the task of comparing the Finnish and Irish Deaf communities is not easy given their cultural and social differences. Nevertheless, the 'import-mirror' approach enables us to evaluate the rate of progress in Ireland. The 'import-mirror' approach also helps us to place Irish social policy responses in an international context.

Finland was chosen because of its similarity to Ireland in key respects. Using the Esping-Andersen model of welfare regimes, it becomes clear that social policy responses to the needs of the Deaf communities are microcosms of national social and economic practices. The Finnish response to the Deaf community bears a strong resemblance to the social democratic model in which stronger state intervention encourages the empowerment of Deaf people to take control of their destiny. In the Irish case, the picture shows a piecemeal and uncoordinated approach to the demands of the Deaf community, a liberal social policy attitude of weaker commitment to egalitarian ideas, and reluctance on the part of the state to intervene on behalf of minorities.

There are some similarities in the historical experiences of the Irish and Finnish Deaf communities. Both have witnessed a long domination of oralism in the education of deaf children, a domination that has left a lasting mark on both communities. Since the 1980s, the experience of both communities began to diverge as the Finns embarked on a positive and democratic approach to development. While the Irish experience has been characterised by slow progress, there have been some positive developments such as the establishment of a representative Deaf organisation, the Irish Deaf Society, and once off, beneficial interpreting and Deaf tutor training courses.

However, things have changed quite dramatically since 2000, undoubtedly helped by a buoyant economy and changes in attitudes towards disabled people in general. Given the persistent campaigning by the Irish Deaf Society, the state eventually agreed to fund a Centre for Deaf Studies and a literacy programme for Deaf people. It also sanctioned the setting up of a bilingual pre-school through the Model School for the Deaf Project and initiated a scheme to have ISL taught to families in their home environments. Moreover, a number of projects aimed at advocacy and literacy are funded by government departments and administered through the Irish Deaf Society (Irish Deaf Journal 2000, 2001, 2003).

The Finnish Deaf community has acted in a cohesive way and has operated a progressive strategy through its representative organisation, the Finnish Association of the Deaf. The strategy involved three policy strands—language policy, education policy and communication policy. The first policy was very successful, and its crowning achievement was state recognition of FinSL and the establishment of the Finnish Sign Language Board. The outcomes in relation to the second strand have been somewhat mixed, since the lack of trained Deaf teachers and the reluctance of hearing teachers to embrace bilingualism hinders full development. However, it must be stressed that the substantive implementation of bilingualism is vindicated by the improvements in literacy levels of deaf children. It is as yet too early to evaluate the third strand, communication policy. Several innovative projects are currently under way aimed at developing services in relation to communication.

In contrast, until relatively recently, Irish Deaf people had developed no clear strategy. Such lack of progress can be explained by referring to the social and cultural conditions of the time. Paternalistic organisations were dominant in providing services and the attitudes arising from this dominance made it difficult for Deaf people to develop alternative approaches. However, with changing social and political circumstances, Ireland may belatedly be able to implement a proactive approach to social policy-making.

We have seen positive and progressive measures introduced to improve the socio-economic status of Deaf people in Finland. Most of the initiatives were based on linguistic and cultural perspectives. The explicit acknowledgement of the Deaf community as a linguistic and cultural minority is identified as an important social and political value. It is clear that lessons can be learnt from the Finnish situation, notably that empowerment of the Deaf community and their participation in policy making are crucial in alleviating the dismal socio-economic situation of many Irish Deaf people.

Notes

1. The Finnish Association of the Deaf forwarded a number of documents and reports, including a report submitted to UNESCO, in a response to my list of questions.

References

Barcham, Lesley. (1998) The International Dimension in S. Gregory *et al* (eds) *Issues in Deaf Education*, London: David Fulton Publishers.

Castles, F. and D. Mitchell. (1993) World of Welfare and Families of Nations, in F. Castles (ed.) *Family of Nations*, Dartmouth: Aldershot.

Chubb, B. (1992) *The Politics and Government in the Republic of Ireland*, London: Longman.

Conama, J. B. and Grehan, C. (2002) *Is there poverty in the deaf community?* Dublin: Irish Deaf Society.

Conama, J. B. (2002) *Tourists in Their Own Lands—A Social Policy Analysis of the Irish Deaf Community's Participation in Society*, unpublished M.Litt thesis, University of Dublin, Trinity College.

Crean, E. (1997) *Breaking the Silence—The Education of the Deaf in Ireland 1816–1996*, Dublin: Irish Deaf Society Publications.

Department of Education (1972) *The Education of Children Who Are Handicapped by Impaired Hearing*, Dublin: Stationery Office.

Esping-Andersen, G. (1990) *The Three Worlds of Welfare Capitalism*, Cambridge: Polity.

Finnish Association of the Deaf (1994) *The Educational Policy Program for the Deaf*, Helsinki: Finnish Association of the Deaf.

—— (1997) *Report from the working group set up by the Finnish Ministry of Justice on the rights of those using sign language*, Helsinki: Finnish Association of the Deaf.

—— (1999a) *Submission No. 002263 to UNESCO—January 10, 1999*, Helsinki: Finnish Association of the Deaf.

—— (1999b) *The Employment Project for Deaf People*, Helsinki: Finnish Association of the Deaf.

—— (2003) *Website*, http://www.kl.Deaf.fi

Hakkarainen, L. (1988) Kuurojen ylaasteen oppilaiden kirjoitetun kielen hallinta, (English translation summary) *Jyvaskyla Studies in Education, Psychology and Social Research* No. 67, Jyvaskyla, Jyvaskylan Yliopisto.

Hietala, M. (1996) From Race Hygiene to Sterilization: The Eugenics Movement in Finland, in G. Broberg and N. Roll-Hansen (eds) *Eugenics and the Welfare State: Sterilization Policy in Denmark, Sweden, Norway and Finland*, East Lansing: Michigan State University Press.

Hill, Michael (1996) *Social Policy: A Comparative Analysis*, Hemel Hempstead: Prentice Hall.

Irish Deaf Society (1997) *Proceedings of a seminar, Bilingual education for deaf children: best option for the future? St. Patrick's College, Drumcondra, Dublin, 22nd March*, Dublin: Irish Deaf Society.

Ireland (2002) Central Statistics Office (CSO), *Website*: www.cso.ie

Irish Deaf Journal (1988), 1(2), Dublin: Irish Deaf Society.

—— (2000), 14(2), Dublin: Irish Deaf Society.

—— (2001), 15(3), Dublin: Irish Deaf Society.

—— (2003), 17(3), Dublin: Irish Deaf Society.

Irish Sign Link (2000) *Unpublished Interim Report*, Dublin: Irish Sign Link.

James, T. and O'Neill, E. (1991) *Reading Assessment of Deaf Children*, Dublin: National Rehabilitation Board.

Kyle, J.G. and Allsop, L. (1997) *Sign On Europe*, Centre for Deaf Studies, University of Bristol.

Lane, H. (1984) *When The Mind Hears: A History of the Deaf*, New York: Random House.

—— (1993) *The Mask of Benevolence: Disabling the Deaf Community*, New York: Vintage Press.

Leibfried, S. (1993) Towards a European Welfare State, in C. Jones (ed.) *New Perspectives on the Welfare State*, pp.133–56, London: Routledge.

Lewis, J. (1992) Gender and the development of welfare regimes, *Journal of European Social Policy*, 2(3):159–73.

Matthews, P. A. (1996) *The Irish Deaf Community: Volume 1*, Dublin: Institiuid Teangeolaiochta Eireann.

May, M. (1998) The role of comparative study, in P. Alcock, A. Erskine and M. May (eds) *The Student's Companion to Social Policy*, Oxford: Blackwell Press.

May, T. (2nd ed.) (1997) *Social Research: Issues, Methods and Process*, Buckingham, UK: Open University Press.

McDonnell, P. (1996) *Verb Categories of Irish Sign Language*, unpublished Ph.D. thesis, University of Dublin, Trinity College.

National Economic and Social Council (1993) *Report No.93 The Irish*

Economy in a Comparative Institutional Perspective, Dublin: NESC.

O'Donnell A. (1999) Comparing welfare states: considering the case of Ireland, in G. Kiely, A. O'Connor, P. Kennedy and S. Quin (eds) *Irish Social Policy in Context*, Dublin: University College Dublin Press.

Organisation for Economic Co-Operation and Development (1999) *OECD Economic Surveys—Finland*, Paris: OECD.

—— *Website*: www.oecd.org

Poverty Today (2002) No 56, September / October, Dublin: Combat Poverty Agency.

Sainsbury, D (1994) *Gendering Welfare States*, London: Sage.

Singleton, F. (2nd ed.) (1998) *A Short History of Finland*, Cambridge: Cambridge University Press.

Swan, E. (1994) *Study on the Dublin Schools for the Deaf*, Privately Commissioned Report, Psychology Department, University College Dublin.

The Model School for the Deaf Project (1998) *Handbook on the Way Forward for Deaf Education*, Dublin: MSDP.

World Federation of the Deaf (1991), in T. Skutnabb-Kangas and R. Phillipson (eds) (1994) *Linguistic Human Rights: Overcoming Linguistic Discrimination*, Berlin: Mouton de Gruyter.

Signs of change in Europe: European developments on the status of signed languages [1]

Lorraine Leeson

> Often individuals and groups are treated unjustly and suppressed by means of language. People who are deprived of linguistic human rights may therefore be prevented from enjoying other human rights, including fair political representation, a fair trial, access to education, access to information and freedom of speech, and maintenance of their cultural heritage (Skutnabb-Kangas 2000: 2).

Introduction

This paper explores the current situation of the indigenous signed languages in Europe, with particular reference to the signed languages of the European Union. The context for this discussion is firmly embedded in the notion that recognition of signed languages brings both freedom from the oppression that has traditionally been associated with use of a signed language throughout Europe (See Fischer and Lane 1993 for a selection of papers concerning elements of this history), and forms the basis for ensuring that other rights that are available to languages recognised by a state or union of states, are also available to signed languages. The practice of deliberately suppressing a language or, more subtly, not supporting the use of a language has been referred to as 'linguistic genocide' (Skutnabb-Kangas 2000). A major step on the road to eradicating attempted linguistic genocide with respect to signed languages is the legal recognition of signed languages and the protection of these languages at international, European and state levels.

Given that this paper takes a European perspective regarding the recognition of signed languages, we begin by briefly describing the major European institutions that play a role in the recognition of signed languages, namely, the European Union and the Council of Europe. We also introduce the non-governmental organisations (NGOs) that represent signed language users across the continent of Europe, again placing specific focus on the European Union NGO, the European Union of the Deaf (EUD). Having described the major European stakeholders, we will outline the international instruments that signed language users refer to in their call for greater recognition and consider the developments that have occurred with respect to the status of signed languages in several European Union states in the period 1997–2003. The reason for identifying this timeframe for consideration is that the first exploration of the status of sign languages across the European Union was carried out in 1997, when the European Commission funded the European Union of the Deaf-led Sign Languages Project (Kyle and Allsop 1997). In 2001, the European Union of the Deaf hosted a meeting of its affiliate organisations of the Deaf to coincide with the opening ceremony of the European Year of Languages activities in Lund, Sweden. Participants were invited to reflect on developments that had occurred for signed language users in the European Union Member States since 1997 (EUD Update, 2001).

Drawing together the major developments that have occurred at European level to date, this paper considers the developing recognition afforded to signed languages and to signed language users across the EU and Council of Europe territories. We also consider the changes that have occurred in how Deaf people view their languages, and critically, their right to use a natural signed language. From a political perspective, we identify the strategies that have been successful in bringing forward the agenda for increased recognition of signed languages at European level, taking the Council of Europe's Charter for Regional or Minority Languages (CRML) as a case study in this regard.

The political context in Europe

The idea of Europe is complex and often defined on the basis of geo-political structures such as membership of the European Union or the Council of Europe. Indeed, many Europeans are not conscious of the presence of the Council of Europe nor of the important role it has in shaping the broader European response to minority languages. In this section then, we will begin by introducing the European Union and the Council of Europe. We will then turn to introduce the European Union of the Deaf, a European Union based non-governmental organisation that represents the interests of the Deaf community at EU level and works with other Deaf community NGOs when consulting with the Council of Europe.

The European Union is a politically defined territory comprising twenty-five member states since May 1st, 2004. These are Austria, Belgium, Cyprus, the Czech Republic, Denmark, Estonia, Finland, France, Germany, Greece, Hungary, Ireland, Italy, Latvia, Lithuania, Luxembourg, Malta, the Netherlands, Poland, Portugal, Slovakia, Slovenia, Spain, Sweden, and the UK.

Regulations governing the workings of the European Union are laid down in the European Treaties, for example, the Amsterdam Treaty (1999). The European Union explicitly states that it values the linguistic and cultural diversity of its Member States. In upholding the motto 'unity in diversity', the European Union maintains eleven official working languages and has, in the past, part-funded the work of the European Bureau for Lesser Used Languages, which seeks to support the indigenous minority and regional languages of the European Union.

As we shall see, the European Union has made reference to signed languages in a number of contexts, most notably in the two Resolutions of the European Parliament regarding sign(ed) languages (1988: 1998). However, more broadly, the Union is working towards a rights based approach to the use of language as an expression of cultural identity. Most recently, this had led to the inclusion, in the Charter of Fundamental Rights, of a reference to the right to freedom to use one's language.

The European Union's Charter of Fundamental Rights, which was signed by the Presidents of the European parliament, the Council, and the Commission of the European Union on 7 December 2000, is historic in that it makes reference to linguistic rights under the banner of an article that deals with non-discrimination. Article 21, paragraph 1 proclaims that:

> Any discrimination based on any ground such as sex, race,

> colour, ethnic or social origin, genetic features, language, religion or belief, political or any other opinion, membership of a national minority, property, birth, disability, age or sexual orientation shall be prohibited.

In signing the Charter the then President of the European Parliament, Mrs. Nicole Fontaine, stated that the charter would be 'a point of reference for all the Parliament acts which have a direct or indirect bearing on the lives of citizens throughout the Union' (www.europarl.eu.int/charter/default_en.htm). Citizens of the European Union now have another document to draw on when lobbying for recognition of their right to use their language.

The Council of Europe territories are also politically defined. The Council has forty-five Member States including many members of the European Union. Since membership comprises states as culturally and linguistically diverse as Russia, Poland, Croatia, Slovakia, the Czech Republic and Turkey, language is an issue which attracts a great deal of attention from the Council of Europe, for example through their Charter for Regional or Minority Languages (CRML 1992). However, given that many of the territories of the Council of Europe have experienced upheaval and war in part as a result of linguistic conflict, there seems to be a tendency to conflate notions of language and nationalism, with the consequence that linguistic rights are often considered in relation to the potential for a linguistic group's potential claim of self-governance. Despite this, Article 14 of the European Convention on Human Rights (1950), which prohibits discrimination, reports that 'The enjoyment of the rights and freedoms set forth in this Convention shall be secured without discrimination on any grounds, such as sex, race, colour, language, religion, political or other opinion, national or social origin, association with a national minority, property, birth or other status' (cited in Afflerbach, 2001: 23). As we shall see, the major components of this article have also been enshrined in other consequent treaties, conventions and charters in Europe, though language has, until recently (with its inclusion in the European Union's Charter of Fundamental Rights), been excluded.[2]

The European Union of the Deaf is a non-governmental organisation of Deaf people representing organisations of Deaf people from across the European Union. The EUD works in partnership with umbrella organisations of Deaf people in Central Europe through the Central European Regional Secretariat of the World Federation of the Deaf (CERS) and in the Eastern Europe/Asia border areas through the Eastern Europe and Middle Asia Regional Secretariat of the World Federation of the Deaf (EEMARS) when consulting with the Council of Europe, given that the territories of the Council include countries represented by these regional secretariats.

The recognition of signed languages is an important pillar in the work of the EUD: since its establishment, the EUD has lobbied for increased recognition of the indigenous signed languages of the European Union. This has culminated in two resolutions on signed languages from the European Parliament (1988, 1998), a resolution on signed languages from the Council of Europe's Parliamentary Assembly (2001), and a further debate in the Council of Europe's Parliamentary Assembly regarding the need to protect signed languages (2003).[3] Each of the resolutions on signed languages, based on the principle of subsidiarity, calls on respective Member States to recognise at national level, the indigenous signed languages of their territories.

At national level, the diversity of legal instruments that protect languages across the Union complicates the issue of recognition of signed languages. While some countries have official languages enshrined in constitutions or laws (e.g. Irish and English are recognised as official languages in the Irish Constitution), other countries do not have a legally official language; for example, English does not have 'official status' because traditionally, linguistic matters were not considered appropriate subjects for State action (Sampson 2001). To bring this example further, we can say that while some countries have constitutions (e.g. Ireland, Greece), others do not (e.g. United Kingdom). This makes it difficult for a European Union-wide call for constitutional recognition of signed languages. However, some countries have attained recognition of their native signed language/s within their constitutions (e.g. Sweden) (Krausnecker 2001). Some countries have already implemented legislation that makes reference to signed languages and the right to a signed language interpreter in a range of settings (e.g. Italy, Ireland, Portugal) (Krausnecker, *ibid*), while others have *de facto* recognition of their languages, as is the case with British Sign Language following the British government's announcements to recognise British Sign Language as a language in its own right, although it currently has no legal status (Federation of Deaf People press release, 18 March 2003).

Given the fact that recognition of signed languages varies from country to country within the European Union,[4] it is not surprising that the EUD has advocated seeking protection for signed languages under the auspices of the Council of Europe's Charter for Regional or Minority Languages, which we will discuss in some detail below. For now, we can note that Sweden, the UK and Denmark have each lobbied for the inclusion of their respective signed languages in their country's ratification of the CRML. None have been successful to date. Lawyers for the Council of Europe argued that signed languages were not natural languages, suggesting that they were 'created' or 'artificial' and that they were not established long enough to be considered 'historically indigenous' to a region or territory. Eminent linguists from across the European Union territories refuted these claims, which in 2000 led to the publication of the Flensburg Recommendations[5] which advocate that in considering signed languages:

> The Council of Europe and other international organisations should consider the desirability and feasibility of preparing a legal instrument to safeguard these languages and the rights of their users. Likewise, the European Commission is requested to sympathetically consider the inclusion of actions to support Sign Languages in their language programmes. (Flensburg Recommendations 2000: Par. 18).

The European Union of the Deaf held a meeting of members in 2001 to consider the path forward for signed languages and the CRML: the question asked was whether the EUD should lobby for inclusion of signed languages under the CRML or for a new treaty that would focus protection on signed languages only. The membership was overwhelmingly in favour of focusing on seeking inclusion of signed languages under the current CRML, perhaps by seeking an annex to the original treaty to allow for those countries who have already signed up to the CRML to ratify the treaty for signed languages. This is the path that the EUD has pursued, though as we shall see, recent developments at the Council of Europe may lead to alternative actions being sought.

 Since then, a number of key players at the European Union have commented publicly that as signed language users consider themselves as linguistic minorities, the European institutions will have to reconsider how they view Deaf communities of signed language users (Mac Pheal, comment at the workshop on the Charter for Regional or Minority Languages, Opening of the European Year of Languages, Lund, Sweden, 2001) To date, no country has included a signed language as one of the languages to be protected under the CRML, but the profile of signed languages and signed language users has risen in the European institutions.

European and international declarations that make reference to signed languages

As mentioned above, there are a number of resolutions on signed languages that have emerged from the European Union and the Council of Europe territories. These include resolutions by both the Parliament of the European Union and the Parliamentary Assembly of the Council of Europe. Here, we can examine the recommendations put forth by each of these documents and consider the implications of such documents at Member State level.

The European Parliament has passed two resolutions regarding the status of signed languages in the European Union. The first resolution was passed on 17 June 1988 and the second on 18 November 1998. In these resolutions, the European Parliament called on the European Commission to put forward a proposal to the Council of the European Union concerning official recognition of the signed languages used by Deaf people in each Member State. Given the founding principle of subsidiarity, it is not possible for the European Union to expressly demand that Member States recognise their national signed languages, though they can (and did) strongly recommend this action at Member State level.

Despite this restriction, through the act of recognising the indigenous signed languages of the European Union as natural languages, the European Parliament's resolutions paved the way for Deaf communities and their supporters to lobby for the official recognition of signed languages at national level. Given the slow rate of change in the status afforded to Deaf people across the European Union, the European

Union of the Deaf lobbied members of the European Parliament to pass a second resolution on signed languages. The 1998 resolution marked the 10th anniversary of the European Parliament's first resolution recognising the indigenous signed languages of the European Union.

Both resolutions called on Member States to officially recognise their indigenous signed languages. Further, they called for the funding of training programmes for tutors of signed languages and signed language interpreters; for an assurance that EU funded programmes (e.g. EQUAL, HORIZON, PRINCE, etc.) would be accessible for Deaf people; that Deaf awareness training be provided for EU officials and for an assurance that public meetings organised by the EU institutions would be accessible to Deaf people by providing signed language interpretation services on request. The complete texts of both the 1988 and the 1998 resolutions can be seen at the European Union of the Deaf website: www.eudnet.org.

Council of Europe's Parliamentary Assembly call for the protection of Signed Languages (2001)

Following a campaign by a United Kingdom member of the Council of Europe's Parliamentary Assembly, Malcolm Bruce, the members of the parliamentary assembly voted in support of a resolution calling for the protection of signed languages in 2001. In its report, the parliamentary assembly called for signed languages to be afforded the same status as spoken regional and minority languages. This call was a result of Bruce's proposal that signed languages be included in a report that was being prepared by the Legal Affairs and Human Rights Committee regarding national minority languages. At the time Bruce noted that this was a significant step forward despite the fact that some members of the assembly were opposed to treating signed languages in the same way as minority spoken languages such as Gaelic or Welsh. Despite this, Bruce reported that he was pleased that the majority of assembly members agreed with him that Deaf people have waited too long for proper recognition of their signed languages (Liberal Democrats News Release 2001).

Further to this call for protection of signed languages, the Report on the Rights of National Minorities (Doc 8920) also included a reference to signed languages, recommending that

> the Committee of Ministers ...(ix) give the various sign[ed] languages utilised in Europe a protection similar to that afforded by the European Charter for Regional or Minority Languages, possibly by means of the adoption of a recommendation to Member States. (Part 1, Paragraph 11)

As we have seen, there has been reluctance to make reference to signed languages under the CRML. As a consequence of this, Bruce and his supporters have advocated the development of an alternative charter that specifically sets out to protect signed languages. To this end, Bruce has again raised the issue of recognition of signed languages at the parliamentary assembly. On 1 October 2003, he raised a question regarding progress towards developing a legal instrument that gives recognition to signed languages in Council of Europe member states. Dudau, Chairman of the Committee of Ministers, stated that:

> The Committee of Ministers is examining initiatives to give sign languages formal recognition. Indeed, it understands the importance of both teaching through sign language and the teaching of sign language as a school discipline. It supports the inclusion of sign languages as a valid economic qualification in mainstream secondary schools.
>
> The Committee of Ministers supports the right to choose the type of school system preferred and welcomes the development of such bilingual school systems and the proposals for teacher training. It also welcomes the training of more interpreters, which, along with the initiatives such as the increased use of subtitles and new technologies, will help to facilitate improved integration of deaf people into society in the workplace and through access to services.
>
> The Committee of Ministers would like to point out an interesting initiative to develop levels of proficiency in sign languages based on the Council of Europe's Common European Framework of Reference for Language now widely used throughout Europe for the definition of language standards.

Bruce went on to thank the Minister for his response but asked that:

> ...he (Mr Dudau) will acknowledge the fact that the Assembly passed by an overwhelming majority a demand that sign language be given official recognition not just in education but in society at large. The deaf community was looking to the Council of Europe to deliver that. When will the Committee of Ministers be able to publish either an instrument or at least a draft instrument that the Assembly may consider?

The Minister responded that the Bureau of the Steering Committee on Education had received a submission from the United Kingdom with respect to this issue and that the Council of Ministers would consider that submission when preparing their response to the Parliamentary Assembly Recommendation 1598 on the 'Protection of Sign languages in the member states of the Council of Europe.'

Clearly this is a topical issue and one that the Council of Europe seems willing to address. It will be interesting to see how a new Charter unfolds and what it will potentially bring to signed language users across Europe. It will also be interesting to note which countries adopt such a charter and whether it will apply to countries that have already formally recognised their signed languages, such as Sweden, Greece and Wallonia (French-speaking Belgium). We should note that this proposed charter is a response to the lack of recognition of signed languages under the Charter for Regional or Minority Languages (CRML) which we discuss in the next section.

The Council of Europe's Charter for Regional or Minority Languages (CRML 1992)

The Council of Europe's Charter for Regional or Minority Languages is a revolutionary charter that aims to protect and promote the indigenous regional or minority languages of Europe. Article 1 of the Charter defines these languages as follows:

(a) 'regional or minority languages' means languages that are:
   (i) traditionally used within a given territory of a State by nationals of that State who form a group numerically smaller than the rest of the State's population; and

(ii) different from the official language(s) of that State;
(iii) it does not include either dialects of the official language(s) of the State or languages of migrants;

(b) 'territory in which the regional or minority language is used' means the geographical area in which the said language is the model of expression of a number of people justifying the adoption of the various protective and promotional measures provided for in this Charter;

(c) 'non-territorial languages' means languages used by nationals of the State which differ from the language or languages used by the rest of the State's population but which, although traditionally used within the territory of the State, cannot be identified with a particular area thereof.'

The CRML offers a range of protection to languages fields such as education, media, law, and public administration. Countries that are signatories to the Charter are required to list the languages that the Charter will cover in their territory. No country has yet included a signed language despite being lobbied to do so.

There are several points worth considering regarding the CRML. When a government adopts the Charter, it undertakes to apply the provisions laid down in Part II of the Charter to all of the duly ratified indigenous languages that are spoken within its territory (the Charter makes specific reference to the 'spoken' nature of these languages). Part II includes (among other things) reference to the need for states ratifying the Charter to formulate policies and legislation on the basis of principles that recognise that regional or minority languages are an expression of cultural wealth which need to be safeguarded. States must also facilitate and encourage the use of ratified languages in public and private life and are encouraged to provide facilities that support the teaching and learning of these languages at all appropriate stages (Article 7—Objectives and Principles).

However, governments adopting the Charter must also apply a minimum of thirty-five paragraphs or sub-paragraphs from Part III of the Charter. These must include at least three paragraphs or sub-paragraphs from Articles 8 and 12 of the Charter and at least one from each of Articles 9,10, 11 and 13. Part III of the CRML is concerned with measures that promote the use of the regional or minority language in public life. Such measures include the establishment of appropriate pre-school, primary, vocational and adult/continuing education in the relevant minority language/s (Article 8), the right to access judicial proceedings via the regional or minority language (Article 9), access to administrative bodies and public services in the minority language (Article 10), the adequate provision of media in the regional or minority language (Article 11), the fostering of cultural activities and facilities that encourage expression in the regional or minority language (Article 12), and the abolition of any discriminatory legal instruments that negatively impact on the regional or minority language (Article 13). However, there are sliding scales of provisions, and, as we noted earlier, governments are not obliged to adopt all measures listed in Part III of the charter. While they must choose thirty-five paragraphs or sub-paragraphs, they are not in any way obliged to introduce the strongest measures that the Charter can provide.

Thus, it is possible that a government's choice of paragraphs in Part III of the Charter will be influenced by economic, social and political factors as well as the guiding wish to offer protection to indigenous minority or regional languages. Regardless of which paragraphs are adopted by a given state, the Council of Europe does police the implementation of the Charter, demanding regular reports from the state regarding the nature of the protections that have been implemented since ratification. Having ratified the charter, a state is obliged to submit a progress report to the Council of Europe within a year. After this point, a report is submitted every three years (Article 15, paragraph 1). All reports are public (Article 15, paragraph 2).

Further, and perhaps most importantly when we come to considering how signed languages have been excluded to date, when ratifying the Charter, governments must specifically state which languages will receive which protections (Article 3, paragraph 1). That is, governments are not obliged to implement the Charter with respect to all of the regional or minority languages that exist in their state: they choose which to include or exclude prior to ratification of the Charter. Equally, they can choose at any time to add another regional or minority language that meets the definitions laid down in Article 1 to their national list of languages offered protection under the CRML

 (Article 3, paragraph 2). As mentioned earlier, much has been made of the fact that the Charter was specifically drawn up to protect spoken minority languages. In fact, it seems that the authors of the Charter were not aware of the situation of signed languages at the time of writing. The fact that the situation of signed languages has become topical in minority language circles is evidenced by the inclusion of a paragraph calling for the need to protect signed languages in the Flensburg Recommendations, though the inclusion of this reference was not uncontroversial (Skuttnabb-Kangas, personal communication 2001).

A final point to note is that the Charter is geared towards protecting languages—not communities of speakers. Indeed, paragraph 11 of the objectives of the charter notes that:

> The charter sets out to protect and promote regional or minority languages, not linguistic minorities. For this reason emphasis is placed on the cultural dimension and the use of a regional or minority language in all the aspects of the life of its speakers. The charter does not establish any individual or collective rights for the speakers of regional or minority languages.

Naturally, the authors of the Charter were aware that protection of language cannot be wholly separated out from the protection of people who use these languages. To this end, they go on to say that:

> ...the obligations of the parties with regard to the status of these languages and the domestic legislation which will have to be introduced in compliance with the charter will have an obvious effect on the situation of the communities concerned and their individual members. (CRML, Paragraph 11, 'objectives of the charter').

As we know, to date no signed language has been recognised and included in a state's ratification of the CRML despite lobbying by Deaf Communities and their allies. They, like the European Union of the Deaf, have argued that signed languages do meet the definitions of regional or minority languages. Leeson (2000:5), writing for the European Union of the Deaf reports that:

> It is important to note here that sign(ed) languages meet the criteria for defining non-territorial languages [...] As sign(ed) languages are typically used throughout the country that they are native to (e.g. Swedish Sign Language in Sweden, Portuguese Sign Language in Portugal), they can be defined as minority non-territorial languages. That is, these are sign languages that are used by people all over the country, but the native sign(ed) language is not the majority language of the country.

She goes on to note that several countries have more than one native signed language, for example, in Belgium, both Flemish Sign Language and Belgian-French Sign Language are used, while in Spain, Spanish Sign Language, Catalonian Sign Language and Galician Sign Language are used.

Further, some countries have signed languages that are regionally based, which complies with the definitions for regional languages as laid down in Article 1. For example, Irish Sign Language is used in Northern Ireland and in very localised areas of the UK. Catalonian Sign Language and Galician Sign Language are also regionally based signed languages in Spain. This is also true for Flemish Sign Language and Belgian-French Sign Language in Belgium. Leeson (2000) notes that these signed languages are used in specific geographical regions by minority signed language users and that these languages are neither the dominant signed languages of the country in question nor the majority language of the country in question.

Despite the publication of paragraph 18 of the Flensburg Recommendations, calling for the safeguarding of signed languages via a legal instrument at Council of Europe level, coupled with public statements from European Commission public servants that the time has perhaps come to recognise that signed languages are minority languages, no signed language has yet been afforded the protection of the CRML. However, with the support of Council of Europe parliamentarian, Malcolm Bruce, the European Union of the Deaf is currently working on the development of a proposal for a Charter on Signed Languages (Helga Stevens, personal communication, November 2003), which will feed into the current work on signed languages being carried out by the Council of Europe's Committee of Ministers.

European Union of the Deaf's 'Sign Languages Project': a 'snapshot' of the status of signed languages in the European Union

In the run-up to the tenth anniversary of the European Parliament's first resolution on signed languages, the EUD sought funding from the European Commission to examine how the status of signed languages had progressed in the intervening years. Research was carried out by the Centre for Deaf Studies at the University of Bristol and published under the title *Sign On Europe* (Kyle and Allsop 1997).

If we summarise the findings of the *Sign On Europe* project, we can say that they reflected a north-south divide. Northern EU countries had a greater awareness and more services than southern EU countries. The research also found that hearing people had more access to information about signed languages and deafness than Deaf people themselves.

Hearing people tended to refer to a service oriented perspective where signed languages were seen as part of a service response to Deaf people who 'needed' that particular 'service.' Organisations also viewed signed language as a need that could be assessed and costed in order to provide support to Deaf people. In contrast, Deaf people's responses implied that signed languages were their preferred languages and that they wished for them to be used and accepted in all spheres of life. Indeed, Deaf people wanted signed languages to be recognised as community languages and expected non-Deaf people to learn and use their languages. Readers are referred to Kyle and Allsop (1997) for a detailed discussion of the issues arising vis-a-vis the status of signed languages across the European Member States in 1997.

The interim period: what has happened since 1997?

The findings of the *Sign On Europe* research were published and presented to the European Commission and the European Parliament. The European Parliament passed the second resolution on sign languages as a result of the findings, which demonstrated that the status of signed languages and their communities of users was not in line with the hopes embedded in the first European Parliament resolution of 1988.

The *Sign On Europe* research was important because, for the first time,

we had a pan-European glimpse of the situation for Deaf people. Most
importantly, Deaf organisations across Europe had been involved in the research. This was a stepping-stone to politicisation. Since this research was conducted, Deaf organisations have been more politically active in striving for recognition of their national signed languages than they were in 1997 (EUD Update, March 2001).

In terms of official recognition of signed languages at national level since 1997, Portugal has recognised Portuguese Sign Language in its constitution (EUD Update, March 2001). Other countries have achieved legal recognition of their signed language. These include Ireland, where the Education Act of 1998 makes reference to Irish Sign Language. Other countries that have established a legal recognition (or whose governments have announced plans to implement such legislation) are Greece (2000), the UK (2003) and Belgian-French Sign Language (2003) (*ibid*). Other countries have neither a legal nor a constitutional basis for the recognition of their signed language/s at present, but often these countries have some kind of *de facto* recognition (e.g. through the provision of sign language interpreters in courts of law, in third level education, etc. despite the absence of a legal basis for this provision) (*ibid*).

Signed Languages as regional or minority languages

As we have seen, the European Deaf community describes itself as a linguistic and cultural group (EUD 1997). Signed language users are seeking recognition, protection and promotion of their languages and cultures on a par with spoken regional or minority languages. As we have noted, the European Union of the Deaf has been lobbying for consideration of this at EU level and with the Council of Europe, and has been successful in raising the profile of signed languages. For example, European Year of Languages (2001) saw signed languages explicitly referred to in publicity prepared by the Council of Europe and the European Commission. Signed language users made their presence felt at the official opening of the European Year of Languages event, challenging the Council of Europe to accept signed languages as legitimate indigenous European languages.

A focused meeting of the European Union of the Deaf followed this event, reviewing the then current status of signed languages throughout the European Union territories and in some non EU states (EUD Update, March 2001). The documentation that provides an overview of the reports delivered by representatives from national associations of Deaf people are listed in the EUD Update, March 2001(www.eudnet.org). This document was subsequently used by the Council of Europe as a starting point for discussing the status of signed languages in their territories, prompting it to seek government reports on this matter. Discussion of signed languages and their right to be protected was also taken up in the Council of Europe's Parliamentary Assembly. There, Malcolm Bruce, MP, raised the issue that signed languages were entitled to the same protections afforded to other minority and regional languages.

There is a growing appreciation of the validity of the view of signed language users as members of minority linguistic communities (e.g. the European Year of Languages activities includes references to signed languages). However, there is no legal basis in the European Union treaties for funding to support regional or minority languages. Also, Deaf people still argue that they are disabled insofar as information and access are denied to them because information is not presented to them in an accessible form (See also Lane 2003 for discussion of this point). European projects that demand mainstreaming approaches do not alleviate this problem, but often serve to isolate people, for example, the cost of interpretation to facilitate signed language users is often significantly greater than that typically allowed for in other cross-European projects where participants may be expected to share a common language/s in order to minimise translation costs.

Other European developments

We have previously made reference to the importance of the Flensburg Recommendations, which offer advice to governments regarding the implementation and application of the Charter for Regional or Minority Languages. As we have noted before, the recommendations include a specific paragraph stating that, like regional and minority spoken languages, signed languages also need to be protected. This is an important advance in terms of lobbying for greater protection of signed languages at Council of Europe level.

As discussed earlier, the Parliamentary Assembly of the Council of

Europe (2001) passed a Report on the Rights of Minorities. This refers to linguistic rights, noting that signed languages need to be offered a protection similar to that offered to spoken regional or minority languages in the Charter for Regional or Minority Languages. In February 2001, the EUD organised a seminar in Lund, Sweden, to co-occur with the official opening of the European Year of Languages. The aim of the seminar was to evaluate progress regarding the recognition of signed languages across Europe since publication of the *Sign On Europe* report (Kyle and Allsop 1997). Generally, the EUD found that:

- There was an increased awareness of the value of signed languages among Deaf communities: signed languages were described by one commentator as 'the jewel in the crown of Deaf culture' (EUD Update, March 2001).
- A changing focus: Markku Jokinen reported that there was debate about the usefulness of the term 'the Deaf person' which focused on the audiological status of a person rather than on her/his language choice. Instead, he proposed the term 'sign language user', which places focus on the language modality preferred by a person (Jokinen 2001).
- Participants reported increased opportunities for bilingual education in Europe, noting that there is a legal right to bilingual education for deaf children in Scandinavia (EUD Update, March 2001).
- Increased demand for learning signed languages: demand currently outstrips supply of appropriately qualified teachers across the European Union. Thus, quality is an issue. Responses to the problem include the establishment of university level training for signed language tutors in many European Union states, including Ireland (EUD Update, March 2001).
- Chronic shortage of appropriately trained signed language interpreters: demand outstrips supply across the European Union. Educational standards of training have increased, but the issue of professional burnout and consequently, turnover of appropriately trained interpreters is a concern (EUD Update, March 2001).

In short, since the *Sign On Europe* research, Deaf people and their organisations were more actively involved in seeking political recognition of their languages at national and regional levels. Within Deaf communities, levels of recognition of the value of signed languages seemed to have increased, with a consequent greater demand that the status of these languages be affirmed politically. Further, more far reaching research would be needed to provide a clearer picture of the reality of the situation for signed language users across the European Union and Council of Europe territories, though it is reassuring to see the European Union of the Deaf take ownership of the task of cataloguing the process of change in the status of signed languages at European Union level. The ongoing task of seeking legal protection for signed language is one that the Deaf communities of Europe are taking very seriously, but it is not one that they must undertake in isolation.

Looking forward: recognising signed languages—drawing on established support

The battle to gain recognition for signed language is not fought in isolation. We have seen that there is an increasing awareness at governmental level across the continent of Europe of the existence of signed languages as legitimate natural languages that should be protected and promoted. We have also seen that preconceived notions regarding the nature of language has precluded success in some quarters: for example, that signed languages should not be included in the CRML because they were considered to be 'artificial' languages. Such claims are demonstrably false given the status of signed language research across the globe at this time.[6]

Inevitably, when seeking political support for recognition of a language, one is asked to provide evidence that other jurisdictions have responded in a similar manner. To this end, local campaigns for recognition of signed languages draw on the experiences of other signed language communities who have successfully gained recognition for their signed languages. Here also, the *Sign On Europe* report and the data collated by the European Union of the Deaf (EUD Update, March 2001) helps. Further, there are international organisations that have also recognised the importance of signed languages.

One such organisation is the United Nations Educational Scientific and Cultural Organisation (UNESCO), which has clearly urged that the signed languages of the world be 'afforded the same status as other linguistic systems.' UNESCO also proposes that signed languages should play an important part in the education of deaf children (Neal-Mahshie 1995, xv). While the World Federation of the Deaf (WFD),[7] a global NGO of Deaf people, continues to lobby for increased global recognition of the important positive role played by signed languages and the fact that access to language is a human right, the support of organisations like UNESCO cannot be underestimated. Such international recognition and support for signed languages is a powerful tool when lobbying for recognition of signed languages at European and national level.

Similarly, the European Parliament resolutions, the Flensburg Recommendations, the inclusion of a reference to signed languages in the Council of Europe's Report on the Rights of National Minorities, and the Council of Europe's Parliamentary Assembly call for signed languages to be given the same recognition as spoken regional and minority languages, all lend weight to national, regional and local campaigns for recognition. Here, international politics can lend weight to local demands and the success of individual communities lends weight to the demand for recognition of signed languages at European and international levels.

How far along the road are we?

Krausnecker (2001:69–70) outlines the following list which summarises the developmental path towards recognition followed by the Roma people in Austria:

Consciousness	The sense of being a group, a minority. Awareness about the need for rights and equal treatment
Single individual becomes active/ an activist	Then organisations are founded, structures of representation created.
Interests are verbalised	Wishes, hopes, demands and needs concerning different levels of society and the state.

Individuals become representatives, leaders	
Part-time staff in organisations	Permanent possibility for contact, questions, etc. is created for other minority members and majority members
Research and clarification	Of legal, political and practical possibilities concerning wishes and needs
Support, help and aid	From individual politicians, civil servants, scientists and majority members
Use of knowledge	Experiences and also structures of other (organised and recognised) minorities
Presence and visibility	In communities, conferences, information campaigns, bodies, boards that touch issues that are the group's issues as well
Positive visibility in society in general	Proud presence (as a result of one's community-internal activities)
Raising of general knowledge about the minority in society	Making use of various ways to transport the 'facts.'
International support	Use experience of one minority in other countries
Internal and foreign affairs	For the question of legal recognition or other big changes, the influence and weight of internal and foreign affairs, Zeitgeist, atmosphere, are enormous: interest from other countries or a need to qualify in human rights standards or a nationalist socialist past will put pressure on a state to act.

Litigation	Use international laws/ conventions to sue for rights. Use national laws.
Intellectualisation of the minority	In the long run: raise the levels of formal education: support the intellectualisation of the minority. This is insurance for the future.

Krausneker suggests that these points could be valid for any minority community seeking recognition, focusing as it does on what a community can do in terms of pragmatic and strategic steps it may undertake on the path towards recognition. In considering the development of the European Union Deaf communities as they seek recognition of their languages, we can state that visibility has increased and that Deaf communities themselves are becoming politically aware of the existence of legal instruments that support signed languages. Deaf people who use a signed language as their first or preferred language are becoming involved in the broader political arena in their own states (e.g. a Belgian Deaf woman has run for senate; an Irish Deaf man is a member of the board of Comhairle, etc.)

Deaf people and their allies are also considering the legislation that exists and it is possible that people may sue for rights that they believe are denied them on the grounds of their linguistic situation. For example, in the field of education, a growing number of parents of deaf children feel that access to Irish Sign Language and a bilingual education is essential to providing an appropriate education for an Irish deaf child. As the right of parents to choose an appropriate education for their child is enshrined in the Education Act, this may be an area where litigation may occur. This is an instance where, despite limited recognition of a language occurring in law, practice often evolves more slowly, and often occurs only when the hand of the law intervenes.

In terms of the intellectualisation of the Deaf community, the final point raised by Krausneker, we can suggest that this is a process that is well underway across Europe. As we have seen, Deaf people are activists, they are leaders (for example through their involvement in the National Associations of Deaf People which comprise the membership of the European Union of the Deaf), and there is a growing number of intellectuals coming to the fore across Europe. Across the continent there are Deaf people who hold postgraduate qualifications in a range of areas and a small but growing number of Deaf people are pursuing doctoral level studies, which frequently entails exploring aspects of their experiences of deafness vis-à-vis other domains (e.g. social policy, equality studies, law, information and communication technology, linguistics, etc.). However, for widespread intellectualisation to be possible, a simple truth remains: recognition of the languages that Deaf people use, together with their families and friends, increases the opportunity for Deaf people across Europe to meet their true potential. Denying their language is not solely a denial of the identity of members of a linguistic community, it is also a denial of opportunity for users of that language to participate fully in society and to contribute to society's development as a whole. Recognition of signed languages paves the way for Deaf communities to fulfil their potential, which, for over a century, has been denied through the suppression of signed languages and the denial that these languages even constitute fully fledged status as languages (for example, Lane 2002, Ladd 1998, McDonnell and Saunders 1993, Kontra, Phillipson, Skutnabb-Kangas and Várady 1999, Skutnabb-Kangas 2000, Fischer and Lane 1993).

Conclusion

In this paper, we have outlined the major developments regarding the recognition of signed languages at European Union and Council of Europe level. We synthesised the resolutions passed by the European Parliament and made reference to the inclusion of a reference to the linguistic rights of Europeans in the Charter of Fundamental Rights—something that signed language users will welcome in their bid to ensure the freedom to use a natural signed language in every aspect of their lives. This paper also provided an overview of developments in the Council of Europe territories, particularly the Deaf community response to the Charter for Regional or Minority Languages and the demand that signed languages be offered protection under the Charter, or be offered protections similar to those available to spoken regional or minority languages. This demand has been echoed in the Council of Europe's Parliamentary Assembly where a call has been made for such protections to be offered to signed languages. This is the current state of play—at present the European Union of the Deaf is working on a draft document that it hopes will influence the form that a Council of Europe charter for the protection of signed languages might eventually take.

We noted that international organisations such as UNESCO were cognisant of the importance that signed languages have in the lives of Deaf communities. Further, we stated that the existence of such international and European documents lends weight to local campaigns for recognition of signed languages.

Notes

1. An earlier version of this paper was presented at Trinity College, Dublin, 8 March 2001.
2. In contrast, while disability has been included in many consequent treaties, charters and conventions that include a non-discrimination clause, it was not included in the European Convention on Human Rights (1950), perhaps reflecting the lack of a cohesive and politically influential disability movement at that time.
3. The texts of these resolutions can be viewed at the European Union of the Deaf website (www.eudnet.org).
4. See the EUD Update March 2001 for a overview of the status of signed languages in each of the European Union Member States. This can be viewed at www.eudnet.org
5. The Flensburg Recommendations set out to guide governments who are in the process of adopting or implementing the Charter for Regional or Minority Languages.
6. For example, see the online International Bibliography of Sign Linguistics at Hamburg University at www.sign-lang.uni-hamburg.de/bibweb/
7. The World Federation of the Deaf's website is: www.wfdnews.org

References

Afflerbach, T. (2001) Protecting and Promoting Human Rights: The Council of Europe and the European Union of the Deaf—Opportunities for Cooperation, in L. Leeson, (ed.) *Looking Forward: the EUD in the 3rd Millennium—The Deaf Citizen in the 21st Century*, Coleford, Glos.: Douglas McLean Publications, 20–33.

Council of Europe (1992) *European Charter for Regional or Minority Languages*, Strasbourg, ETS 148: 5.XI.1992.

European Centre for Minority Languages (2001) *Flensburg*

Recommendations on the Implementation of Policy Measures for Regional or Minority Langauges, Flensburg, Germany, ECMI.

European Union of the Deaf (1997) *The Guide: A European Guide to the Deaf Community*, Brussels: European Union of the Deaf.

—— (2000) *EUD Update, April, Gent Conference Proceedings*, Brussels: EUD (www.eud.net.org).

—— (2001) *EUD Update, March, Update on the Status of Sign Languages in the European Union*, Brussels: EUD.

—— (2001) *EUD Update: Special Issue to Commemorate the EUD Sign Languages Day held on 6 December 2001 at the European Parliament to mark the closing of the European Year of Languages. Vol. 5, No. 5. Special Issues*, Brussels: EUD.

Fischer, R. and Lane, H. (eds) (1993) *Looking Back: A Reader on the History of Deaf Communities and their Sign Languages*, Hamburg: Signum Verlag.

Fromkin V., Rodman, R. and Hyams, N. (7th ed.) (2003) *An Introduction to Language*, Boston: Thomson Heinle Publishers.

Jokinen, M. (2001) 'The Sign Language Person'—A Term to Describe Us and Our Future More Clearly?, in L. Leeson (ed.) op. cit. 50–63.

Kontra, M., Phillipson, R., Skutnabb-Kangas, T. and Várady, T. (eds) (1999) *Language: A Right and a Resource—Approaching Linguistic Human Rights*, Budapest: Central European University Press.

Krausneker, V. (2001) Sign Languages of Europe-Future Chances, in L. Leeson (ed.) *Looking Forward: EUD in the 3rd Millennium—The Deaf Citizen in the 21st Century*, Coleford, Glos.: Douglas McLean Publications, 64–73.

Kyle, J.G. and Allsop, L. (1997): *Sign On Europe*. Centre for Deaf Studies, University of Bristol.

Ladd, P. (1998) *In Search of Deafhood: Towards an Understanding of British Deaf Culture*, unpublished doctoral dissertation, Centre for Deaf Studies, University of Bristol.

Lane, H. (2002) Do Deaf People Have a Disability? *Sign Language Studies*, 2(4):356–379.

Leeson, L. (1997) *Sign On Europe Project: An Interim Report. Paper presented as part of the 'open lectures' series*. Centre for Language and Communication Studies, Trinity College, Dublin.

—— (2000) *Towards an Inclusive Multi-linguistic Europe for All: Making the Sign Languages of Europe Visible in the Council of Europe's Charter for*

Regional or Minority Languages 1992, Brussels: European Union of the Deaf.

McDonnell, P. and Saunders, H. (1993) Sit on Your Hands: Strategies to Prevent Signing, in R. Fischer and H. Lane (eds) *Looking Back: A Reader on the History of Deaf Communities and their Sign Languages*, Hamburg: Signum Verlag, 255–260.

Neal-Mahshie, S. (1995) *Educating Deaf Children Bilingually*, Washington DC: Gallaudet University Press.

Sampson, Geoffrey (2001) What is a Minority Language? *Elsnews: The Newsletter of the European Network in Human Language Technologies, special edition on minority languages*, Spring, 9–10.

Skutnabb-Kangas, T. (2000) *Linguistic Genocide in Education or Worldwide Diversity and Human Rights*, Mahweh, NJ: Lawrence Erlbaum Associates.

Stevens, H. (1997) *EUD Sign Languages Project 1996–7: A Summary Report of the National Committees final Reports*, Brussels: European Union of the Deaf.

Supalla, T., Bergmann, R., Denmark, C., Jokinen, M., Schroeder, O., and Suwanarat, M. (undated) *Report on the Status of Sign Language*, Helsinki: World Federation of the Deaf.

Other Documents

These documents can be downloaded at the following email addresses:

The Amsterdam Treaty (1999): http://europa.eu.int/abc/obj/amst/en/

The European Charter for Regional or Minority Languages (1992): http://www.coe.fr/eng/legaltxt/148e.htm

The European Convention on Human Rights (1950): http://www.coe.fr/eng/legaltxt/5e.htm

European Union Charter of Fundamental Rights (2000): http://www.europarl.eu.int/charter/default_en.htm

Report on the Rights of National Minorities (prepared by the Committee on Legal Affairs and Human Rights) (Doc 8920) (2001): www.areekhelsinkin.ar/bhr/english/index.html

Contributors

David Breslin is secretary of the Deaf Heritage Centre in St. Joseph's, Cabra, Dublin. He has a particular interest in the lost history of Deaf people in Ireland and through his research, especially in the field of art, has discovered many forgotten names. He acts as a guide for Deaf visitors to the National Gallery and has lectured extensively on the history of Deaf artists in Ireland.

John Bosco Conama is chairperson of the Irish Deaf Society and is active on many committees and working groups within the Civil Service and other government bodies monitoring the progress of Deaf and disabled people in society. His first post-graduate work focused on social policy and the Deaf community and recent publications include research on poverty within the Deaf community. He is currently working towards a PhD in Equality Studies in University College Dublin.

Dawn Duffin worked as a teacher in the UK before moving to Dublin in 1994. After meeting Deaf students for the first time in the National Training and Development Institute at Roslyn Park College, she began to research ISL in Trinity College Dublin. She now works as NTDI's co-ordinator for Inclusive Education at Blanchardstown where she manages projects to support students in mainstream education and continues to research in the area of deafness and English literacy.

Susan Foley-Cave is a part-time lecturer in interpreting at the Centre for Deaf Studies, Trinity College Dublin, where she also coordinates reading support. She has worked in an extensive range of interpreting environments since qualifying as an interpreter in 1999. Her research interests include Deaf culture, identity politics, interpreting, ethics and power. Her most recent research focused on Deaf humour and she is currently working towards an M. Litt in Sociology.

Carmel Grehan is a full time member of staff at the Centre for Deaf Studies, Trinity College Dublin, and is also a College Tutor. She is interested in curriculum development and teaching methodology. She has worked in the Deaf community in a number of contexts, most recently on an Irish Deaf Society/Combat Poverty research project. Other recent publications include a paper on the role of gender in contemporary ISL (co-authored with Lorraine Leeson).

Lorraine Leeson is Director of the Centre for Deaf Studies at Trinity College Dublin. She has worked with the Deaf community in a variety of contexts at national and European level, and in both Irish and UK universities as an interpreter trainer. She has particular research interests in sign linguistics and interpreting and has published widely in these fields. She is currently working on a corpus-based description of ISL and a textbook on signed language interpreting.

Patrick A. Matthews is a Senior Lecturer at the Centre for Deaf Studies, Trinity College Dublin. He has played a key role in the Deaf community with an extensive knowledge and experience of teaching ISL in a variety of contexts. Recent publications include a demographic study of the Irish Deaf community, a structural linguistic account of ISL as well as a number of other papers. He is currently working on his PhD at Trinity College Dublin.

Joe McDonnell is a teacher in a school for Deaf pupils in Dublin. He lectures on Bilingualism in Education and Society at the Centre for Deaf Studies, Trinity College Dublin, and is currently researching the relationship between this subject and deafness. The kind of language planning required to meet the linguistic needs of Deaf people in Ireland is one of his particular interests.

Patrick McDonnell teaches in a school for Deaf pupils in Dublin and is a part-time lecturer in the Centre for Deaf Studies, Trinity College, and in the Education and Equality Studies Departments at University College Dublin. He has researched and published extensively on Deaf Studies, Equality Studies and on special education. His most recent work is a study of the relationship between disability and society in Ireland.

 Helena Saunders holds an M.Phil in Applied Linguistics from Trinity College Dublin as well as Certificates in Equality Studies from University College Dublin and in Deaf Studies from the University of Bristol. She is founder of Handwords which provides ISL teaching in schools and colleges and to families in their homes. She specialises in one to one or small group tuition and in developing sign language proficiency in deaf infants and young children.

Index

HOME OF

Douglas McLean

PUBLISHING

FOREST BOOKS

Other deaf studies titles from Douglas McLean

DEAF IDENTITIES
G. Taylor & A. Darby (Eds.)
This is a collection of inspiring and moving contributions from a wide range of Deaf people that reflect radically changing times. The rising level of awareness of the needs of Deaf people, and the discrimination and oppression they still face, is mirrored by the many changes within the Deaf community. Significantly, the rise in 'mainstreaming' of deaf children, cochlear implantation, political activity for rights all represent a considerable challenge to the static notion of deafness and deaf people's cultural identity. Deaf Identities is essential reading for all studying or interested in deaf issues, but it is also an enlightening and enjoyable read for anyone.
£18.95 Paperback 272 pages 2003 ISBN 0 946252 53 X

SIGN LANGUAGE INTERPRETING: Linguistic Coping Strategies
Jemina Napier
This book analyses how sign language interpreters use their translation style and make particular omissions as potential strategies for coping with the linguistic challenges they face when interpreting. Based on a particular study, the findings can also be applied in many different interpreting contexts and the book offers a new way of thinking about interpreting challenges and of how interpreters best meet the needs of their target audience. It also offers a new taxonomy for the analysis of omissions and omission types.
£19.95 Paperback 224 pages 2002 ISBN 0 946252 37 8

INTERPRETING INTERPRETING: Studies and Reflections on Sign Language Interpreting
F Harrington, G H Turner
This book demonstrates current thought and practice within the profession and is an important reference for students and working interpreters. Two major sections focus on issues relating to the structure of the profession and underlying principles of service provision, and on interpreting practices within health care, education and the law. Informed throughout by the perspectives of a range of Deaf and hearing collaborators, the authors discuss material arising from extensive involvement in the delivery, management and analysis of interpreting services, and draw upon primary research experience.
£16.95 Paperback 128 pages 2001 ISBN 0 946252 48 3

DEAF WORLDS - INTERNATIONAL JOURNAL OF DEAF STUDIES
This international journal provides a focus for analysis and debate on social, psychological, cultural and political factors influencing the lives of deaf people and the societies in which they live.
Deaf Worlds is published three times a year in March, July and November as a quality journal aimed at students, professionals and everyone with a serious interest in deafness and deaf issues.
For current subscription rates, please see www.forestbooks.com, Or contact the distributor below

Distributed by Forest Book Services
Ellwood Road, Coleford, Glos., UK, GL16 7LE
Tel +44[0]1594 833858 (voice/text) Fax +44[0]1594 833446